The Angel of Mostar

Sally Becker

The Angel of Mostar

One Woman's Fight to Rescue Children in Bosnia

HUTCHINSON
London

This edition first published in 1994 by Hutchinson

Random House UK Ltd
20 Vauxhall Bridge Road, London SW1V 2SA

Random House Australia (Pty) Ltd
20 Alfred Street, Milsons Point, Sydney, NSW 2061, Australia

Random House New Zealand Ltd
18 Poland Road, Glenfield, Auckland 10, New Zealand

Random House South Africa (Pty) Ltd
PO Box 337, Bergvlei, 2012, South Africa

ISBN 0 09 178927 3

A CIP catalogue record for this book is available from the British Library

Set in Perpetua by Deltatype Ltd, Ellesmere Port, Cheshire
Printed and bound in Great Britain by Clays Ltd, St Ives PLC

For the children

Whom shall I send, and who will go for us?
Then said I, Here am I; send me.

Isaiah Chapter 6, verse 8

CONTENTS

CONTENTS

ILLUSTRATIONS

ACKNOWLEDGMENTS

With special thanks to the following people: My mother and father, Bas Radford, Jenny Rose and all my family for their support. Duncan Stewart, my knight in shining armour. Brigadier Dr Ivan Bagaric and the Croatian Military Health Authorities for making everything possible. Vava, my great friend and protector. Lynne Gillette, for being there. Collette, who will never be forgotten, and Sean. Zoran, a hero. Hafid, the neurosurgeon whose concern gave me strength. Damir, Stipe and Erna Rosic. Mike and Jennifer Mendoza for their absolute faith in me and their constant hard work on my behalf. Roger Ferris, Gloria Macari, Yolanda Beeny and Graham Boyd and all the people who were involved with fund raising, especially Chayla, Alex and all the children. Justine, Val, Karen and Stuart. June Jacobs. Joyce Simpson. Eva Mitchell. JACS. UKJAID. ICJW. Michael Harris, Professor T. Scarlet Epstein, Ansel Harris, Rabbi Dr Jeremy Collick, Lana Kay and The Hove Reform Synagogue. The Immam. The Bosnian Information Centre, London. The Sir Halley Stewart Trust. Norris McWhirter. George Urban. Paddy Ashdown. *The Sunday Mirror* Appeal. Heartlands Hospital. Lawrence Le Carre and the volunteers of Operation Angel. The Veterans for Peace. Brian Lee of Barclays Bank. John Dyer, Ron Waight and Andrew Popkeiwicz. Barbara Haywood and Brian Charig. Sally Line Ferries. Brighton Collective Group of Hotels. The AA and BRS. The Life Foundation. The rescue services, the Police and the Territorial Army. Sphere Drake.

My thanks also to all those in the media who reported with fairness and accuracy, and in particular the following people for their help and support in the war zone. Mark Dowdney of *The Daily Mirror*, Christopher Morris of Sky News, Brent Sadler of CNN and Robin White of ITN.

I would also like to thank UNPROFOR soldiers and aid workers in Bosnia who risk their lives for others every day, especially Major Need, Colonel Peter Williams, Major Tohler, Sonja Thompson and Danielle.

And to all the individuals too numerous to mention for their help, encouragement and support.

And to my literary agent, Vernon Futerman.

And lastly to my editor, Tom Gilliatt, for his patience and understanding and to everyone at Hutchinson.

With sincere thanks to Liz Gill for her invaluable help.

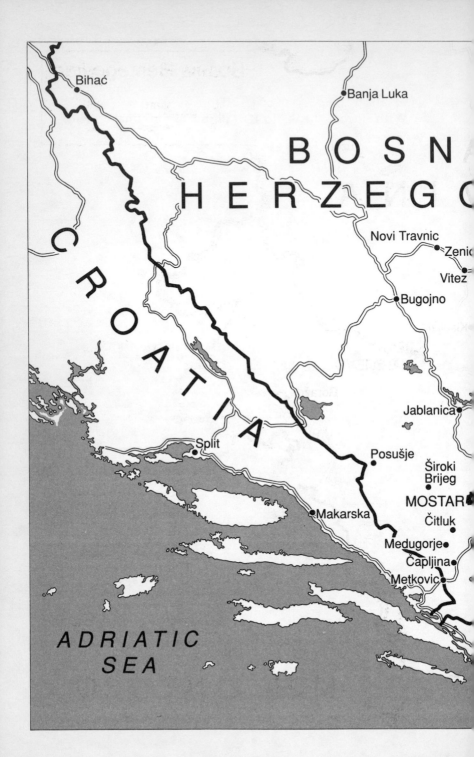

PART ONE

Sunflowers and Snipers

1

CROSSING THE LINE

This was as far as the police escort would come. From this point we were on our own. Behind me lay the relative safety of the little Croatian town of Čitluk which had been my home in recent weeks. Ahead lay the war-torn city of Mostar, its West side under Croatian control, its Muslim East besieged for the past four months. During that time its people had been under almost constant fire; now their children were dying for want of the most basic medical supplies.

My task was to drive a rickety old Bedford ambulance into the hospital there and bring those sick and wounded children out and back to a United Nations base. From there they could be flown to safety and specialist care. But first I had to face the unknown terrors of no man's land.

I had spent countless hours planning and preparing for this mission: hours of begging for supplies; hustling for documentation; pleading, sometimes arguing, with the authorities to unravel their red tape and let someone do something. Now at last the moment was here. However afraid, I felt there could be no going back.

I was wearing a pair of jeans and a white T-shirt in the hope

3

that white would show any distant sniper I was not a soldier. I carried a holdall with spare underwear, torch, toothbrush and washbag and a bottle of vitamins in case I should become trapped in the city like the UN aid convoy which had gone in the previous day and which, I had just heard, was now being prevented from leaving by a crowd of desperate townsfolk.

I had phoned my mother before leaving Čitluk and told her I had been given permission to go to East Mostar to help some children. I did not want her to know how dangerous the journey might be so I had not elaborated. Later she was to tell people I had made it sound as casual as going on a shopping expedition which is exactly what she had done after talking to me. 'Sally called, she's popping over to East Mostar today, something to do with kids,' she told her sister. 'Oh, really,' replied my aunt unconcernedly as they wandered around Marks and Spencer in Hove.

I sat at the wheel of the ambulance. In the back were the vital supplies as well as the coffee, cheese and cigarettes which the hard-pressed doctors and nurses craved. Beside me in the passenger seat was a slightly built, balding man called Paul whom I had agreed to take with me at the last minute. He had been hanging around our hotel for a while, trying without success to get permission to cross the line to see friends but his own vehicle had recently been confiscated. As soon as he heard I was going he begged to come along. He claimed he would be a great help: he spoke the language, knew the route and had connections on the east side. His arguments made sense and, though I was not without my doubts, I said yes.

A ceasefire had been arranged between the Muslims and Croats. It would last until 1pm the following day. There remained however the question of snipers positioned in the city and within a four kilometre radius around it. The thought that these maverick marksmen might not have heard of our agreement did little for my confidence.

Dr Ivan Bagaric, a brigadier in the Bosnian Croat army, HVO, head of the military health authorities and the man who had made my mission possible, came to see me off from Čitluk. As he hugged me someone translated his words: 'I will pray for you,' and I could see the fear and concern in his eyes. I knew he was worried for my safety as a friend and for his own reputation which was on the line politically. After all what he was authorising was the rescue of enemy children and in the bitter battle for Mostar, a city emotionally and strategically important to all sides, there were many who did not distinguish between combatants and civilians.

Two Croatian policemen escorted us to the front line via a steep track down the mountain side to a disused airport. Having previously driven only to West Mostar this route was unfamiliar to me and Paul alarmed me further when he said he had never been this way either. He was worryingly ineffectual when I asked him to translate directions from the departing police. Eventually I managed to make myself understood and one of them drew me a rough map although of course he could not give me any guarantees as to its accuracy: he had not been beyond this point since hostilities began.

The television crew which had been behind us all the way could likewise go no further but they filmed us setting off and as I pulled away across the deserted runway I kept hoping no sniper would decide to take a pot shot at them. The press were widely disliked in this area and several had been killed.

I drove as fast as I could across the runway. It was hot and humid and I had to slide the door back just to get a breath of air. We were the only thing moving for miles and I knew we were within the sights of both sides. The thought of how many eyes might be watching us made me cringe and yet it was a beautiful evening with the sun still shining brightly and the mountains visible all around us in the clear light. As we turned left on to the main road I spotted a sign to Sarajevo and tried to picture what this road must have been like only a couple of years before when it was teeming with traffic and people going about their everyday business.

Now the road was eerily quiet apart from the odd thump of a distant shell and empty except for the mines whose deadly spikes protruded from the tarmac. I steered around them, Paul silent beside me. After a few moments I turned right up a track as the map indicated towards a railway barrier where three soldiers were waiting. They were in their early twenties and were wearing very worn khaki shirts and trousers and had old trainers instead of boots but they still had rifles slung across their shoulders. I showed my documents to the one who seemed to be in charge but he simply stared at it blankly. He muttered something in his own language and I turned to Paul.

'I think he said they don't know anything about this,' he said. I was not impressed.

'Well did he or didn't he? Could you be more specific?' But Paul merely shrugged. I reached under my seat and gave the soldiers a carton of cigarettes which obviously pleased them.

'Mostar?' I asked, spreading my hands to show my ignorance. The soldiers pointed towards the city and gestured that I should follow the road I was on. I felt like Dorothy from *The Wizard of Oz* when she was told to follow the yellow brick road. Hoping to lighten the atmosphere I said to Paul 'We're not in Kansas any more Toto.' He did not laugh.

Within minutes we were at the outskirts and passing houses from which children began to emerge. As we drove on more and more people came out on to the road, calling for cigarettes and chocolate. I stopped the ambulance and handed out some but almost immediately we were surrounded by a throng and I realised we had better press on.

We turned another bend and the road became a pot-holed track. I negotiated a narrow gap beneath a small bridge and as we emerged from the other side I had my first glimpse of my destination. Mostar lay ahead of us, nestling at the foot of the mountains. The west side appeared as a geometric mass of bright modern high rise blocks and spacious shopping centres. In sharp contrast was the eastern side of the city where crooked but pretty houses with terracotta roofs and moss-covered grey brick walls lay in higgledy piggledy fashion on the hillside leading down to the river Neretva. So close together are they that during the fighting people used each other's kitchens and living rooms as cut-through routes to avoid snipers. By the time I was there this had become such an accepted practice that the inhabitants would not even look up from their cooking as you darted through.

From a distance the city looked peaceful, only the odd puff of smoke indicating the shelling taking place on either side. For two years Mostar had been pounded by Serbian artillery fire. More recently the fighting between Muslims and Croats had divided the city leaving the Muslim East side besieged by the West.

Before the war it was regarded as one of the jewels of central Europe and a favourite haunt of tourists who would pay local children to dive off the old bridge spanning the river between the east and west sides. Now these children were dying for want of the most basic medical supplies.

Suddenly I heard a loud noise close by and realised with horror that we were being shot at. Where the hell was this ceasefire we had been promised? Paul dived on to the floor while I tried to throw away my cigarette, close the door and change gear all at the same time. We were still in first gear but the gear lever was too far away for me to reach it and stay under cover at the same time so I jammed my foot to the floor and with the engine roaring in protest weaved to and fro hoping to confuse our attackers.

The shots came one after another. I was terrified to the core of my being, convinced I would be killed at any moment. My life did not flash in front of my eyes; all I could think was what a waste my death would be after all the trouble I had had getting the permission to go in. I felt sure the man shooting at the ambulance would not be doing so if he knew I had come to save his children.

I drove as fast as first gear allowed, alternately ducking below the steering wheel and popping up to check where I was going. I could feel the thumping of my own heartbeat and I was whispering 'please, please' over and over again like some form of prayer. As soon as I could change gear I accelerated away until I reached the cover of the first buildings. It must have taken only ten minutes but it felt like ten hours.

I have been asked many times since whether I got a 'buzz' from such experiences and the answer is – not for one moment. In fact I think anyone who does get a buzz from being shot at needs their head examined. Excitement was the last thing I felt: I wanted to weep with fear and frustration; I thought I would never see anyone I loved ever again; I wanted to stop and hide until all the baddies had gone away.

Instead I drove slowly past the buildings, speeding up at

each junction where the road came into full view of the surrounding territory. Then I saw the way ahead was blocked by an overturned truck and behind it was a long line of white trucks belonging to the Overseas Development Administration (ODA). Alongside them was their UN escort in armoured vehicles. I pulled up, my hands shaking and my leg aching from the pressure I had used to accelerate. Paul stepped down and moved off to find his friends and I cannot say I was sorry to lose him.

I locked the ambulance and began to walk towards the convoy. Again I was surrounded by people clamouring for cigarettes and coffee. They were pale and thin but they did not seem to be starving as we had feared. The situation felt surreal: there was I wandering along in my jeans and T-shirt, there were the UN forces with their flak jackets and blue helmets. Their jaws dropped with surprise when they saw me.

Several stepped forward including Albert Benabou, the UN's civil affairs officer whom I had dealt with on several occasions. He clapped me on the back.

'I knew you would come,' he said

I turned away angrily to confront Leo, a UN policeman and in fact one of the main instigators of my trip. It was his original request that I use my Croatian contacts to facilitate the evacuation of one particular little boy that had triggered the mission.

'I've been shot at almost all the way in,' I shouted. 'What's going on?'

He looked unhappy and apologised. 'I'm sorry,' he said. 'I couldn't tell anyone you were coming because I wasn't able to leave my Armoured Personnel Carrier.'

'Well, what about Droce Azem,' I asked. This was the little

boy in urgent need of a heart operation whom Leo had asked me to rescue.

His answer stunned me. 'He died twenty-two days ago.' I felt devastated. I was only thankful I had been granted permission to bring other children out as well.

A Spanish captain drove me to the hospital through the dangerous side streets. It was an immense relief to be able to put my life in someone else's hands. I was tired of the responsibility.

The hospital was built of red brick, its walls pockmarked by shrapnel and bullets and its windows blocked up with sandbags and wood. It was dark now and I had to use my torch to find my way to the basement and the doctors.

The smell grew stronger as we descended the stairs: sweet and cloying and overwhelming, the stench of blood and putrefaction. I had never smelled anything like it before but I knew it was the smell of death.

The floor squelched under my feet as I picked my way in the dim light along the underground corridor of a building which had once been a public health centre in a thriving city but which was now a makeshift hospital in a devastated war zone.

Around me there was a frenzy of movement and noise as exhausted doctors and nurses, often near to panic, struggled to deal with the flow of sick and wounded against seemingly impossible odds. The walls of the corridor were lined with patients awaiting emergency surgery. They lay on stretchers, trolleys, old tables, anything that could be pressed into service, and the drips in their arms dangled from hat stands. Many moaned or screamed in pain; others lay still with a frightening resignation. It seemed like a production line in hell.

A young woman from ITN asked me if I would be filmed

meeting my evacuees. 'It's a wonderful story,' she enthused. 'A whole convoy trapped and you come in and rescue sick children.' I said I did not mind if the children did not. I stepped through an arch into a room and what I saw there will haunt me forever, for this was the children's ward, crowded with the innocent victims of a conflict not of their making and beyond their comprehension. They had been hit by shells or sniper fire or mines or rocket attacks, sometimes in their own homes, other times as they ran a desperate errand for their families or snatched a few moments play in the streets as they did in the days of peace. The oldest was barely seventeen, the youngest a toddler.

Lying in one of the many beds was a little girl named Selma Handzjar. Her face was swollen and completely distorted by black holes where the shrapnel had hit her. Lying in the next bed was her younger brother. Their mother sat between them. 'Selma was beautiful,' she cried, 'why her?'

I went over to Selma, who spoke very good English, and took her hand. 'I've come to take you away from here to somewhere safe and quiet,' I said softly. 'No more bullets, no more shelling. Somewhere peaceful where doctors can make you beautiful again in no time.' She smiled at me and then to my horror threw back the sheet which had been covering her and waved with the tiny stump of what had once been her arm. I tried desperately not to let her know how upset I was but she must have sensed it. 'Don't worry,' she said, her turn now to reassure me, 'it's nothing.'

At that moment I was filled with shame for all those times when I had moaned about a headache, a toothache or some other trivial complaint, and filled too with admiration for this brave little soul who was trying to make light of her appalling

11

injuries in order that I might feel better. And more than that I realised that in some terrible way such a tragedy was part of her normal life. She had seen friends suffer similar traumas and worse. What for me seemed a living nightmare had become for her an everyday reality.

Her brother called to me in a loud voice: '*Kiri iki.*'

A nurse translated: 'He's asking for peanuts, they're his favourite.'

'Tell him he'll have peanuts and chocolate and anything else he wants if I've got anything to do with it,' I said and I fought back the tears as I walked away from them and towards all the other beds.

The doctors were enormously grateful for the supplies I had been able to hand over. Even the simplest things were almost priceless in an area where nothing could be brought in. Prior to the latest ODA convoy there had only been one delivery of aid and that had been sixty-seven days ago; even the 200 tons that had just arrived would only relieve the situation for a short time.

Word of my arrival spread quickly. On my return to the UN group Albert Benabou drew me to one side. 'We are trying to arrange the release of the convoy in return for the evacuation of the children,' he declared.

Still shaken by the scenes in the hospital I rounded on him. 'How dare you? When I asked for UN assistance no one wanted to know, yet now you're in trouble you're prepared to use the children.'

He answered in a voice as angry as mine. 'Don't you understand? Everyone is in danger here. There has been a lot of shelling. There is no food and water. The population are desperate. They could turn on the aid workers and the soldiers at any minute. Your evacuation might be the only chance we have.'

I thought for a moment. It was too dark now to risk leaving with the children so his negotiations could not make much difference. If I had to leave without the convoy it would be safer in the morning.

Albert tried another tack. 'Look, we have doctors, we have an ambulance. You cannot safely put five or six children plus a couple of mothers in the back of one vehicle. We also have helicopters on standby at Medugorje to fly the patients to Zagreb.'

'OK.' I said. 'Negotiate. I'll wait.'

He went off but after two hours of talks it was clear he was getting nowhere. There was no sign of the convoy being allowed to leave and tempers were getting frayed. I spent the time being interviewed by the press and the TV crews who had gone in with the UN and were now trapped with them.

I went back to my ambulance to wait. Brent Sadler from CNN and his camerawoman joined me. He stretched out on the floor, oblivious to the thuds and bangs around us, not even waking when a shell exploded on the other side of the small hospital car park, but I was unable to sleep.

I took my torch and went back down to the basement where the doctors still sat, talking and smoking their precious cigarettes. I was introduced to a slight, gentle man in his forties called Hafid who was the only neurosurgeon in East Mostar. Serious and sad, with intense dark eyes and a nervous manner, he told me how he and his colleagues averaged twenty operations a day in appalling conditions. There was, for instance, no ordinary oxygen supply: instead they relied on oxygen normally used for industrial purposes. Amputations were performed where in other circumstances a limb might have been saved.

Many of his patients had been forced out of West Mostar across the ancient bridge into the east putting extra strain on the scant resources. As for the city, that lay in ruins. Out of seventeen mosques only two remained. There was no running water or electricity and people were forced to chop up their furniture for fuel to cook and boil water. The front lines were no more than ten metres apart in some places so the enemy was literally half a street away.

His wife, who was living on the other side, was pregnant with their first child and he was deeply concerned about her, not just because she was a Muslim like him and thus in danger, but also because she suffered from endometriosis which could be hazardous in childbirth.

He asked if I would take a letter to her and suddenly several other doctors wanted the same. I told them to write their letters but to put their names and addresses inside the envelopes in case they fell into the wrong hands despite my care. The worst message I was asked to deliver was from a doctor who wanted me to phone his brother in Germany and tell him his wife had been killed.

Around three o'clock in the morning I was joined by the Spanish captain and we stood at the hospital entrance and talked against the background hum of the oil-fired generator, the building's only source of power.

'Have you managed to persuade them to let the convoy go with you?' he asked.

I shook my head. 'My ceasefire ends at lunchtime. I'll wait until eleven to give you time to talk to the Muslim commanders but then I must leave, otherwise it will be too dangerous. The Croats are expecting me, they know my ambulance is full of children. They won't shoot as long as I arrive within the given time.'

The captain did not look too happy as he walked away.

At dawn I was interviewed live for BBC's *Today* programme by Jeremy Bowen who introduced me down the satellite phone with the words 'There has been an amazing turn of events. Sally Becker, a freelance aid worker, has arrived in Mostar to evacuate wounded children and the United Nations are hoping to use this evacuation to come out on her tail.'

Some of the press had asked me to try and arrange for their vehicles to accompany mine when I left. Many had urgent stories to file; some were simply afraid. I explained to the doctors that these people were civilians and no use as protection to anyone. They agreed.

At eleven o'clock there was still no sign of movement from the UN and we began to carry the children to the ambulances. As I bent down to help lift Selma inside I remembered a quotation: 'No man is taller than he who stoops to help a child.' As I saw the happiness shining from her face I felt like a giant.

Suddenly a car screeched into the compound. It had no glass in the windows, its bodywork was scarred with bullet holes and on its side was daubed a crude red cross. I watched in horror as two small boys of three and five were carried from the back. Their bodies were covered in a film of blood and they writhed and screamed in agony. Behind them a woman who appeared to be in a state of severe shock was being led from the car carrying a newborn baby girl with shrapnel wounds to her face and leg.

I thought what I had witnessed in the children's ward was appalling but this was even more dreadful. The sight of those tiny bodies with their unspeakable injuries was the worst thing I had ever seen. As soon as the way was clear I ran into the hospital asking what we could do for them. A doctor told me he could stabilise them in two or three days – if they lived.

'Would you come back to get them?' he asked. 'It might be their only chance. The eldest has terrible stomach wounds and we don't have enough antibiotics to combat infection. The younger boy will lose his sight if he is not operated on quickly.'

'Of course I'll come back,' I promised him, the mother's face still seared on to my mind. To have one child in pain is a nightmare for any mother and here were three with the most horrifying wounds. Her husband was leaning against the vehicle with his head in his hands, distraught with grief. I would bring the mother out too, I vowed to the doctor and he took my hand and squeezed it.

'You are a very special person, Sally Becker,' he said and he turned to rejoin his team. Tears ran freely down my cheeks as I left the hospital. This war was an obscenity.

Inside my ambulance we tried to make the children as comfortable as possible. Brent and his camerawoman climbed into the front beside me. They had no car and I had agreed to give them a lift. Paul had reappeared and he squeezed in beside a child. To my disgust he lit a cigarette and we all called to him to put it out at once. He was an odd man: good-hearted and brave enough to cross a war zone just to see friends but thoughtless and unrealistic in other ways.

We pulled out of the car park and I waited for the UN ambulance carrying the other children to join us. Five, ten minutes ticked away and still there was no sign. Brent got out and went off to see what was causing the delay. The sun beat down fiercely on the ambulance roof and the children moaned in discomfort. Thank goodness I had had the foresight to bring a bottle of water along.

Finally Brent reappeared with Albert and Leo. 'They say you can't leave without the convoy,' he said.

'What do they intend to do,' I asked, 'Hold us hostage?'

It seemed incredible that they should even consider delaying the evacuation of seriously injured children as a means of breaking their own deadlock. I was outraged and told Albert so.

'You have to have co-ordination,' he insisted.

By this time Brent and other TV crews who had been waiting to join us had begun filming the argument. Suddenly Albert's boss Cedric Thornberry arrived on the scene and I marched angrily towards him to explain what was happening. When I returned to the ambulance I was approached by an old Spanish officer with a long brown beard who made me think of Rumpelstiltskin. Rudely he ordered me out of my vehicle.

I told him the ambulance did not belong to him and had been loaned to me by the Croats but he failed to understand and stood there gesticulating and shouting. One of the children cried out in pain and the women looked terrified. I kept telling Paul to reassure them in his limited Serbo-Croat though I felt far from reassured myself.

Albert reappeared and told us we could not leave with the promised UN ambulance as it might be needed for soldiers. We would either have to take the other patients ourselves or leave them at the hospital. Our choice was to endanger the children further by crowding them into one vehicle or tell some they could not leave after all. Either option was completely unthinkable.

What was more, Albert said, there would be no helicopters waiting: they had been cancelled the night before. My head spun. There I was parked beside a sniper's alley in the blazing heat, in an ambulance filled with wounded children, with a ceasefire that would end in forty minutes and still the UN were determined to use me as some sort of blackmail threat. I knew the people of East Mostar were equally desperate. They wanted UN protection and holding the convoy was the only way they could think of to get it. For them my evacuation was a separate issue. I felt I was in the middle of a bad dream from which there was no escape.

Finally my patience snapped. As I prepared to confront Thornberry again Albert stepped in. 'It's OK,' he said. 'You can go, and the other ambulance can go with you. There's been a misunderstanding.'

I received no explanation for the sudden reversal and at that moment I did not care. All I felt was relief.

We drove away through the ruined streets followed by the second ambulance and four press and TV vehicles. Suddenly a man appeared hobbling along in front of us on crutches. It was Selma's father making sure the people on the streets did not impede his wife and daughter's progress to safety.

Not one shot was fired on the return journey: both sides now knew of the ceasefire. Even so I did not allow myself even a silent cheer until we reached the far side of the old airport. But the moment we crossed the line and I knew we were safe emotion welled up inside me. It was indescribable. I was filled with happiness and a great sense of pride. It was the most important moment of my whole life and everything that had gone before, both good and bad, had been leading up to it.

2

NO ANGEL

What makes us what we are? Perhaps it is genetic. Certainly there were one or two colourful characters in my family, including my great grandfather Edward Emanuel, who, as founder of the Bookmakers' Protection Association, mixed with the highest and lowest in London society.

He was a man who was on first name terms with Winston Churchill and who once accepted a pair of Edward VIII's cufflinks as a gambling stake but who had so many enemies that he needed a bodyguard to protect him. He was also one of the Jewish leaders who used to break up Oswald Mosley's Black Shirt meetings during the rise of British fascism in the Thirties. He made a fortune but gave it away almost as fast, mainly to Jewish refugees fleeing the Nazis. Another branch of the family produced a complete contrast to Edward in the devout rabbi and judge, the Reverend Dayan Spiers.

Yet my parents Jack and Carol were conventional enough. My father ran a small finance company and we moved to Hove on the south coast from London when I was very small. We were an ordinary, middle class family, and my parents were loving and generous to me and Eddy my brother and two sisters

Elaine and Wendy.

I remember being particularly close to my grandmother, Edward Emanuel's daughter, who was a strong-minded woman and believed I could do or be anything I wanted. Parents with four children cannot be singling out any one for special attention but I think the fact that my grandmother believed in me so completely and was so totally loyal to me – my father used to say that if I was standing over a body with a smoking gun she would argue my innocence – helped enormously with my self-confidence.

I used to run around with a gang of boys from our street. Not a gang in the sense that strikes fear into people's hearts nowadays but a group of nice boys who had included me in their football, rugby and cricket almost since the day we moved in and they came to spy on the new family and perhaps indulge in a bit of teasing. At the age of four, I am told, I had marched towards them with my chin jutting and shouted 'Sticks and stones may break my bones but names will never hurt me,' a piece of repartee which I had just learned.

I was a total tomboy. Indeed the day one of them pointed out 'You've got bosoms' was a terrible moment for me: somehow I had always thought I was the same as them. I never cared for dolls, except Action Man types and when I was taken to Hamley's as a special treat I picked a cowboy outfit rather than a nurse's uniform. Years later when people in Bosnia mistook me for a nurse I would remember that and smile to myself.

I cannot say religion was a moving force in my life. My grandparents kept Shabat and we were all members of the Hove Reform Synagogue but I rapidly became disillusioned when I realised that boys had bar mitzvahs, with their coming to manhood marked by gifts and great rejoicing, unlike most girls. The male was revered far more than the female, especially by the Orthodox. It was my first real experience of sexism.

That is not to say I am an atheist. I believe in God as creator and that we are all here for a purpose. I think of myself as a spiritual person but I have never had much interest in the trappings of religion and after Bosnia, where I saw what people were doing to each other in the name of religion, I have even less. My attitude has always been: why pray about a problem if you can do something practical about it?

Perhaps being Jewish, however, has some relevance. My father made me read a lot about the Holocaust when I was growing up and I was always tormented by the question: if I had been alive then would I have helped? Bosnia answered the question for me. I know now that I would have fought back, would not have let myself be ushered into the ovens. Though no doubt they might have shot me long before.

I went to a mixed junior school but then to an all-girls secondary which did not suit me, though I was well enough liked, partly because I used to mess around and make everyone laugh.

I had no appetite for a nine-to-five job so when I left school with five 'O' levels and 'A' level art I went over to Israel to work on a kibbutz. I loved it there and although, as I say, I never had much time for religion, I did experience what many Jews feel when they get there: that I had in some way 'come home'. All those stories of Moses and the like which had previously seemed on a par with fairy tales suddenly became real.

What I liked about the kibbutz was that it encouraged

21

individualism and at the same time gave complete equality to men and women. I felt I had found my niche, that I was free and in control with no one telling me what to do all the time. It also gave me my first experience of war and an insight into an aspect of my character that was to re-emerge years later in Bosnia.

The kibbutz had come under attack in an air raid and we had all taken cover in an air-raid shelter. Volunteers were needed to run to the dining rooms to fetch food and water for the rest. I offered to go and raced across the compound. When I got back everyone was congratulating me and although I did not think I had done anything special it gave me a warm feeling to know other people thought so. They were admiring me for something I considered normal and I realised that I was not frightened by many of the things that frighten others. I am not saying I was courageous, simply that I do not remember being at all afraid.

I came to know fear in Bosnia and I think the difference was that there I knew I was a target, that the gunmen were shooting at *me*. But in the Israel days I still lived in a storybook world. I was a great romantic and thought life should be like it is in books and the movies.

For the next three years I was involved in a relationship with my first love, Uri Eshkoli, who I met on the Kibbutz Kfar Giladi. He was an incredible man, intelligent, humorous and very popular. Uri had served in the Israeli army, a hero of the 1967 Arab-Israeli war and was seriously injured fighting at Suez. A piece of shrapnel hit him in the back and paralysed him from the waist down. He was only twenty-three when it happened and despite the fact that before his wound he had been incredibly physically active (he would scale the wall of a building rather than enter through the front door), he bravely faced up to a future confined to a wheelchair and crutches and worked hard, running the kibbutz quarry on the Golan Heights.

After the kibbutz I worked in the Hilton Hotel art gallery in Tel Aviv and then got the job of manager of the Omar Khayam night club in Old Jaffa. My boss was the singer and comedian Joel Sharr, owner of the club and star of its cabaret. I was infatuated with him despite the fact that he was much older than I and looked like the devil from a pantomime.

But the pay was poor and despite working long hours through the night I could not make enough to support myself. I decided therefore to return to Britain for a few months to earn some more money. Unfortunately, and to my everlasting and bitter regret, I became involved with a group on the drugs scene. I had never been interested in drugs myself – I liked being in control too much and besides my highs came naturally – but I was caught with a quantity of cannabis.

It was my first offence but they wanted to make an example of me and I served four months in prison for it. First I was on bail for a year, waiting for the case to come to court, my passport was confiscated and I had to report twice daily to my local police station. That in itself had felt like imprisonment but the sentence itself was truly terrible. It deprived me of my self-respect as well as my freedom. It was also my first encounter with 'The System' as I came up against the rigidity of bureaucracy with its endless rules and regulations which could never be broken, never even stretched, however urgent or complex the situation. It was a phenomenon I was to witness again and again in Bosnia during my battles with officialdom.

In prison I met people who were locked away for what

seemed to me ridiculous reasons. One woman was mentally retarded with the mind of a child yet she was serving two months for stealing soft toys. A young girl, a product of Borstal, was there because she had nowhere else to go and would re-offend in order to have some security. I remember an old woman scrubbing floors for eight hours a day with swollen arthritic fingers: her 'crime' had been failure to pay her rates.

There was also a woman there from the year above me at school. Lorraine was beautiful, intelligent and amusing but she suffered from depression and other psychological problems which caused her to lash out violently in frustration. But instead of being treated she was forever being dragged to the punishment block. We became friends as I listened to her tales of the past but although she seemed happier, it was too late. The board decided to transfer her to another prison.

The decision sent her into such a frenzy that the officers actually put manacles on her. As we said goodbye I could see tears glistening in her large brown eyes. The following day a warder brought me a box: Lorraine had left me her belongings. With great sadness I sifted through the contents: a few trinkets, a hair band, a paper doll and, most moving of all, a poem which spoke of loss and loneliness. Shortly afterwards I learned that she had committed suicide.

I became something of a rebel. The prison staff were striking for better pay and as a result each woman was locked up alone in her cell for twenty-three hours a day. I hated it, hour after hour with no one to talk to, nothing to do but stare at the bars. Several times I refused to be locked in and on one occasion my skull was fractured in the struggle to get me inside. If it had not been for the kindness and understanding of one particular officer I believe I would have gone the same way as Lorraine.

My sentence was short but it felt like a lifetime. It did however teach me one important lesson: you cannot beat 'The System', you can only try to survive it.

After my release I spent the next year frantically trying to get a job, any job, with the help of a local policewoman who was also a close friend. Unfortunately every application form asked about previous convictions and since I always answered honestly I was always turned down. Finally, in despair with my country, I decided to try my luck abroad. I moved to Austria where I had a friend and made my living turning out portraits, usually of children, sometimes at the rate of one a day.

I then spent a couple of years in property development in the South of France where a Brighton company were planning a golf course complex. Originally I was taken on to help design the interior of its hotel but as the months went by I found myself increasingly involved in the business side, dealing with bankers and planning officers and the like. The project eventually foundered and I found myself once again without a job. I had, however, gained valuable negotiating experience and the confidence to face up to powerful men which were to stand me in good stead when I came to deal with the authorities in Bosnia.

The money side of work has never mattered much to me. I have never been a saver: if I have had it, I have spent it. In Austria I lived in a bedsitter. In France if I had notes I would buy a good dinner; when they ran out I would go through the flat picking up all the loose change I had scattered about until I had enough for a loaf of bread.

People often think that because of what I did in Bosnia I must be a rugged, stoical individual who enjoys roughing it. On the contrary, I like my comforts very much, I am picky about my food and essentially lazy: if I had had to walk across the front line I would never have gone. I have never been practical. When my school trip climbed Ben Nevis I would not wear hiking boots because I did not like the look of them and went up in my pumps. Twenty years later I would be sinking into the mud of Mostar in my sneakers while everyone else was sensibly shod. And I hate extremes: whereas someone else is cold, I am freezing and instead of just being hungry I am starving. Tough I am not.

Back home again I found myself simply whiling away time, all too frequently in the local pub. Only the Gulf War was able to galvanise me. I saw on the news that peace protestors were planning to set up camp between the Allies and the Iraqis and I was filled with admiration. After all, most of us think war is something way above us and beyond our control yet here were ordinary people trying to have an extraordinary effect.

I found their headquarters, packed my bags and within two days was on a plane to the Middle East. Because I was Jewish it was thought my presence might put others at risk – I could be seen as a spy or seized as a hostage – so it was agreed I would stay in Amman in Jordan and deal with the press.

When war did break out the protestors were trapped. My response was to send a hand-written fax to Queen Noor asking for help in the belief that if you need something done you should start at the top. My instinct paid off: the queen arranged for two buses to go to the border where we could pick them up and I went with the escort. The only time I felt in any danger was when an Iraqi guard climbed into my car and began questioning me. All I could think of was to give the thumbs up sign and make loud noises of approval whenever he mentioned Saddam Hussein and the opposite response when he said Bush. It worked.

On my return to Britain I met Polly Perkins, the singer and actress who was about to play one of the leading characters in the new BBC soap *Eldorado*, set in southern Spain. She was intrigued by the fact that I had just come back from a war zone and invited me over to her villa near Mijas to paint. I had a wonderful time there, painting male and female nudes, seventeen of which were shown in an exhibition, supporting myself by appearing as an extra in the ill-fated soap opera.

By then the world was becoming aware of the conflict in the former Yugoslavia and I was increasingly aware of a desire to do something to help over there. I had however acquired a little dog by then whom I loved dearly and, as Polly and my other friends pointed out, I had a responsibility to him.

Then several things happened. My dog was run over and killed, *Eldorado* was scrapped and an Aids benefit concert I had arranged back in Brighton was a flop. Admittedly we had been over-ambitious and booked too large a venue but all the artists wanted payment and I lost any money I had had.

As I grew ever more disillusioned with what I saw as the crass materialism all around me, the scale of the suffering in Bosnia began to emerge. Night after night the television news would be full of harrowing pictures and I watched with mounting concern.

I cared little about the soldiers, they at least had some choice in the matter. It was the innocent victims, particularly the children, who so distressed me. I cannot say I have ever been a wildly maternal person but I always got on well with children and adored my two nephews, Joby, Max and his baby sister Katy.

I had in fact been at Katy's birth, vowing as my sister moaned in labour that I would never go through it myself, and had been the first to hold her. Holding a new baby makes you think of the spiritual side of life and as I watched those scenes on television I was haunted by the contrast between Katy, Max and Joby, loved, wanted, warm, well fed, and those children in Bosnia who were loved as much but who were homeless and hungry, wounded and dying.

On the night of my thirty-third birthday I was watching the latest footage of Bosnia's agony when I suddenly realised that I had nothing to lose: no home of my own, no money, no husband or children, no lover, not even a dog any more. Of course I had friends and family but none of them was dependent on me. I was free to go.

3

INTO THE UNKNOWN

'You can't get insurance for dismemberment,' called my father from the hall. I continued putting the last few items in my holdall, wondering if I had overlooked anything of vital importance: it is not easy packing for a war zone. A couple of dog tags engraved with my blood group, given to me for luck by a friend, were the last items. We would be travelling to Bosnia by road through Europe without any overnight stops. I had been told to bring a sleeping bag, cup, plate, knife, fork and spoon. I also had a bag of toys donated by local people and my guitar.

A third bag held an assortment of sketch books, paints and crayons as Suncokret, the only aid organisation operating in Bosnia which had accepted me (all the others I had applied to had rejected me because of my lack of medical qualifications), had done so because of my experience as an artist. Suncokret, sunflower in Serbo-Croatian, provided volunteers for refugee camps in Croatia and Bosnia Herzegovina to assist in various aspects of camp life. My job would be to help children use artistic expression as a way of working through the traumas they had suffered. I had never done anything like this before but at least it was a start.

My parents had reacted differently when I told them I was going. My mother was worried about the dangers I might face, living and working in a war zone, but she accepted my decision, knowing how upset I had been by all the images of suffering we had seen. My father, however, thought I had lost my marbles and that I had no inkling of what could happen to me out there. He kept trying to dissuade me with tales of rape and the dreadful wounds artillery fire causes. As it happens my greatest nightmare from childhood has always been the loss of a limb and I would shudder whenever he brought the subject up.

When at last I went to say goodbye to him he was in the lounge watching television. As I approached his chair he held up a dark object, opening it to display a wicked looking blade. 'It's a killing knife,' he stated sombrely and proceeded to demonstrate its locking device.

'Carry it with you always, you never know when you might need it.'

'I couldn't kill anyone,' I said.

'But you might need to use it in self-defence,' he persisted.

Seeing that it would make him feel better if he thought I had some protection, I agreed to take it though I knew in my mind I would probably only ever use it for cutting up food. As I left the room I heard him call 'Good luck.'

A friend had agreed to drive me to the rendezvous point and my mother insisted on coming along to see me off. My sense of adventure mounted as I counted at least ten large, white-painted vehicles with red crosses at the front and back waiting in the car park.

Such convoys left here every month funded by the Medugorje Appeal, a charity named after the small village in Herzegovina which had become a world-famous place of pilgrimage ever since a group of children claimed to have seen visions of the Virgin Mary there. I was being given a lift along with two other Suncokret volunteers. The rest of the travellers were truck drivers, co-drivers and pilgrims.

We parked the car and carried my bags into a very large, dimly lit room packed from floor to ceiling with humanitarian aid: boxes of tinned food, flour, medical supplies, mattresses, blankets and clothes of all kinds. Suddenly my mother began to cry and I saw that she was looking at a small stack of green army stretchers, a sight she had not seen since the Second World War and which brought home to her the seriousness of what I had embarked upon.

I comforted her by making her laugh and reminding her I would be home again in a couple of weeks. None the less guilt welled up inside me at the thought of her worrying about me while I was away. The official length of stay for Suncokret was three weeks; after this, depending on how much of an asset the volunteer had been, the period could be extended by the same length again.

The work would be unpaid but food and board were provided. I had only my return train fare and a small amount of spending money. I kissed my mother and my friend goodbye, not wanting my mother to be disturbed further by what she might see or hear. I smiled and waved as they drove away, tyring to conceal the doubts and fears lurking beneath my excitement.

Later that evening a briefing was given by a man of my own age called Martin. His hair was cropped short, military-style, and he had a broad grin which seemed to spread from ear to ear. Martin had served in the British Army for ten years before working as a self-employed mechanic in between running the Appeal's convoys.

He explained the situation in Bosnia as well as he could considering its enormous complexity. The war, we were told, had begun two years earlier when the Bosnian Serbs launched an offensive against the Bosnian Croats and Bosnian Muslims with the aim of creating a 'Greater Serbia'.

The victims were then driven out of their homes by the thousand to become refugees or thrown into concentration camps where they might be beaten, raped, even killed. This was the infamous 'ethnic cleansing' process whose horrors we had been seeing on television. Most of the men, women and children who were suffering in this way were Muslims though many Croats were victims too.

Around the time of my first trip the situation was changing again. Croats and Muslims who had previously fought side by side against a common enemy were now beginning to fight each other and, as with all civil wars, friends found themselves fighting friends; neighbours who had once lived in harmony were now bitter adversaries; even families were divided merely because in the past a member may have married someone who now turned out to be 'the enemy'.

Both sides had formed volunteer armies to defend themselves: the predominantly Roman Catholic Croats were the HVO, the Muslims the BIH, although to confuse the picture even further, in areas which remained united against the Serbs, Muslims would fight with the HVO and Croats with the BIH. Later on I was to learn that neither Croats nor Muslims seemed to know who started the conflict between them though inevitably each blamed the other.

Certainly in Mostar, for example, which had already suffered a Serbian onslaught, thousands of Muslims had been rounded up by Croats and driven into camps or across the front line which by then divided the city in two. At the same time nearly 200,000 Croats had been 'cleansed' from central Bosnia by both Serbs and Muslims. Many of those who survived had fled south and were living in and around Medugorje.

The Croatian port of Split which was our first destination in the former Yugoslavia was, said Martin, teeming with refugees from almost every part of the country. They were the displaced and dispossessed whose homes had been burned to the ground, whose cherished belongings had gone for ever. These were the people, regardless of ethnic background, that I was hoping to help in whatever way I could and as I listened to him my determination became stronger than ever.

The following morning, 16 May 1993, after loading the trucks via a human chain from the warehouse and hearing Mass (those of us who were non-believers stood to one side), we set off. The journey, through France and Italy down to Ancona where we were to catch the ferry to Split, was long and arduous but despite the discomfort I managed a few hours sleep and felt both refreshed and elated as we sailed into the beautiful Adriatic seaport.

Almost as soon as we docked I became aware of the refugees, mostly elderly women dressed in black, their heads covered with scarves leaving only their eyes to reveal the horrors they had witnessed. Many had lost husbands and children either through separation or death. They pleaded with us for money. I tried to give a few dinar, the local currency, to one woman but I was immediately assailed by others. There was no way I could afford to help them all so I rejoined the convoy personnel who were clearing customs and passport control.

We drove along the coast of Croatia towards Bosnia Herzegovina passing through an idyllic succession of resorts with the sea calm and the brightest of blues: it seemed inconceivable that battles were raging less than an hour away. Even Medugorje, just ten miles away from Mostar, seemed virtually untouched by the war.

The main street was dominated by a large church and overlooked at the far end by the hill known as the Hill of Crosses which pilgrims, often barefoot, would climb through the heat, stopping to pray at each Station of the Cross. The only clue to the conflict was the fact that street signs were peppered with bullet holes where soldiers had used them for target practice.

The next day we travelled in convoy to Posušje, a town about an hour and a half away where the bulk of our aid was to be delivered to a school housing more than 200 Muslim refugees. The building itself was filthy and most of the refugees were lice-ridden. There had also been a recent outbreak of hepatitis A which the Red Cross had only just managed to contain. This camp was run by a small dedicated group of Italian volunteers who were dishing out a pasta lunch when we arrived.

The refugees ate at long wooden tables in a dark grim room. The building had no electricity and hardly any water and people slept twenty to a room crammed in upon mattresses on the floor. I went to talk to an old woman and her brother, known in the camp as Mama and Baba. Mama insisted I drank the sweet syrupy Turkish coffee so popular in the area as she told me her story. I listened aghast as a young girl translated.

The Serbs, or Chetniks (Serbian extremists) as she called them, had reached her village and begun to clear each house systematically, either forcing the inhabitants out at gunpoint or flushing them out by setting fire to their homes. Many had been burned alive, trapped in the basements where they had sought refuge. The young men had been taken away to camps but Mama's husband and son had been shot in front of her. Tears welled up in her eyes and rolled down her wrinkled cheeks as she spoke.

I wanted so much to give her something, something to bring her at least a glimmer of hope for the future, to show that people still cared. All I had was a small gold ring in the shape of a heart with a tiny diamond at its centre. I passed it to her and she smiled through the tears. Almost in desperation she tried to push the ring on to her finger but it would not slide over her swollen old joints. I took off the thin gold chain I'd always worn around my neck, threaded the ring on to it and fastened it around her neck. She was fingering it lovingly as I said goodbye, tears in my own eyes, tears of frustration and rage as well as sympathy.

Here was a simple old woman forced to watch the murder of her loved ones who were guilty of nothing more than coming from the 'wrong' ethnic background. How could human beings be capable of such barbarity? It was a question I was to ask myself many times over the next few months.

Outside the camp I found some of the volunteers drinking beer at a drab little bar. Sitting with them was a sixteen-year-old boy called Seemo who, I noticed when he grinned at me from behind his hand, had no teeth. Seemo, someone explained, had been captured and taken to a Chetnik concentration camp with his parents: his brother and sister had disappeared. At the camp he was tortured, both his arms were broken and all his teeth smashed. Yet he remained the playboy of the refugee camp, always flirting with the female volunteers.

Someone suggested I draw his portrait and so I went to the truck to search through my belongings. As I did so a boy appeared. This was Aldo, he was eight years old and he had seen his entire family murdered. He rarely spoke and almost never smiled. I offered him a cuddly toy from the sack of things I had been given in Brighton but he shook his head and backed away. He also declined a handful of lollipops. On impulse I reached for the guitar I had brought with me. His face lit up but he was still watching me suspiciously as he edged into the truck.

Gently I settled the guitar into his small hands and watched his expression change from fear to peace as he stroked the instrument. Take it, I indicated, but he shook his head vehemently and pushed it away. The distrust had returned. Once again I placed it in his arms and he took it. As he raced back into the building I saw that the guitar was almost as big as his thin little body.

I returned to the bar with my sketch pad and proceeded to draw Seemo's portrait. He could hardly sit still he was so excited by the prospect of seeing himself on paper but I noticed that each time he remembered to pose he would clamp his lips together so that I should not catch him with a toothless smile. When I finished I handed him the sheet of paper and he beamed with pride as he held it up for everyone to see.

The other two Suncokret volunteers who had travelled with me were to stay on at Posušje. One was a carpenter and devout Catholic who had spent the previous day climbing the Hill of Crosses, the other a fair-headed youth who had come to Bosnia on the advice of his parents: apparently he had been involved with a bad crowd and they thought the experience might change his attitude. Shy and kind he had brought football and cricket gear with him and seemed the perfect type to work with traumatised children. I wished them both luck.

That evening we drove back to the guest house in Medugorje and as night fell I stood on my balcony to watch the orange light of tracer bullets streak across the surrounding hills. I could hear the distant thumps of shells from the direction of Mostar and I shivered though the night air was warm.

Early next morning I went over to the Pax Hotel which housed refugees, mostly Catholics, from both the Serbian onslaught and from the Croat/Muslim conflict in Mostar. Marina, the woman who acted as their unofficial leader, was a typical example. She had left West Mostar in 1992 but after five months with relatives in Split had decided to return with her nine-year-old son and his four-year-old sister.

Within minutes of their return there was an air raid. Her neighbour's two children were killed: they were the same age as her own. It was then that she decided to leave the city for good. Her husband, however, was responsible for the water supply and would remain, despite the fact that his salary for the past year had never been more than the equivalent of £40 a month. He and other husbands, most of whom were fighting for the HVO, would try and visit their wives and children twice a month. Other women were less fortunate: either their men were dead or their whereabouts were unknown.

There were sixty-three children at the Pax Hotel when I arrived, three of whom had been born in the past few months. On the whole the women were friendly and helpful to each other but the atmosphere was often uneasy and the one Muslim among them was beginning to sense hostility as news of fighting between Muslim and Croat filtered through to the camp. Each family had one small room – not bad for a mother and one child but cramped for numbers above that – but, compared to Posušje, the Pax was luxurious.

The women worked in whatever way they could to earn money. Although foreign aid was able to supply one meal a day the women were short of all those everyday things we take for granted: toiletries, Tampax, disposable nappies, feeding bottles and vitamins.

As I looked round the well-equipped kindergarten I realised that art therapy for the children was less essential than making life easier for their mothers. And I knew that I wanted to do much more than play with the children, especially as none of them seemed traumatised in the way the children in Posušje were.

Marina and I drank coffee in the hotel reception area and I was introduced to the receptionist's brother, a handsome young man who should have been studying for a career, instead of fighting for his life and those of his family. As he talked to me about the war he grew more and more angry about the plight of his people and began to shout at the lack of interest from the West, particularly the USA and Britain.

Almost weeping with frustration he hurled figures at me: the numbers of Croatian deaths, the numbers ethnically cleansed from central Bosnia. For him I represented the nations who had abandoned Bosnia Herzegovina. I had no answers for him, only suggesting that now the West might finally intervene. 'It's too late,' he cried, 'two years too late.'

A smart middle-aged woman approached our table and Marina explained she was the hotel owner. I told her how wonderful I thought it was that she gave up her income to house the refugees but she shrugged and said, 'What else could I do? Leave my own people to sleep in the streets?' When Marina told her that I had come to work at the Pax she startled me by suddenly leaning forward in her chair and seizing my arm.

'You are not for this, you have more serious things to do.'
I turned to Marina. 'She's right,' I said. 'I do feel I have to do more than this. You need so much here and others need even more. I want to go back to England with a list of your needs. I want to bring you enough to last so you don't have to spend all your time worrying how to survive.'

The woman with whom I was to share a room had noticed the pack of Tarot cards amongst my belongings and both she and Marina begged me to give them a reading. I had never taken them seriously and I was loth to read for women who had such serious matters to deal with. But before I left I finally agreed and in order not to offend the others who were all devout Catholics we locked the door.

Marina's cards were pretty basic, hard work and lots of responsibility. There was also a card denoting disappointment. She told me that she had been promised a place for herself and her children in Italy and she supposed that the people who had built up her hopes would let her down.

My room-mate Renata, however, had wonderful cards: an unexpected surprise, happiness, romance, love. She laughed ruefully: 'No chance of that. I haven't seen my husband for five months. He's been fighting for the HVO in Mostar but he's Muslim, so I doubt I'll ever see him again.'

That afternoon as I gathered my things together to return to Britain a man knocked on the door. He was wearing camouflage uniform and asked for Renata. She was outside with the children so I called to her from the window. She came to the door and as she saw the man her mouth opened and her eyes widened. She looked from him to me. 'My husband,' she said and ran to him. I closed the door carefully behind me to give them their privacy.

4

A CRESCENT, A CROSS AND A STAR

When I told Martin of my decision and asked for a lift home he offered to let me co-drive his own eight ton truck. The return journey was much quicker than the outward as we had left most of the vehicles behind, bringing back only Martin's truck and the red bus which carried the other drivers and pilgrims. A further convoy was scheduled to leave Godstone two weeks later and I had been assured of a place. I planned to spend the next fortnight collecting as many of the supplies on my list as possible.

Dr Duncan Stewart, a local GP and long-time family friend, put together a large box of medical supplies, including antibiotics and painkillers and a sterilising unit which I knew would be invaluable to one of the hospitals. Family and friends began asking around for baby clothes, toys and blankets while I assembled packages of toiletries and other items Marina had requested.

I tried explaining how desperate the situation had become out there but I was disappointed to find that many people did not want to know. I spoke a couple of times on Radio Sussex, my local station, and I phoned many companies in the area with requests for surgical instruments, feeding bottles, nappies and anything else which could be useful but always I received the same reply: 'We've given our quota to charity already.' However, despite such a lack of interest I was still able to collect many boxes of vital supplies within those two weeks.

This time my family were happier about my leaving and much more supportive. It was a combination of the fact that I had returned home safely and their new knowledge of the terrible suffering I had seen.

I had been taken on as a driver for this convoy and when I reached the warehouse I was told I would be driving the red bus with a volunteer called Sean as my co-driver. Sean was in his mid-twenties, tall and slim with brooding good looks, olive skin and cropped black hair. His ambition was to become a photographer and he planned to use the journey to assemble a portfolio.

Sean gave me a quick driving lesson in the car park but when we hit the road I still felt as if I had no idea what I was doing. I could not get any feel for the length of the vehicle and felt as if I were taking up the whole road. I was driving by the seat of my pants but I must have been doing something right for by the time we got to France I not only felt confident, I loved it.

I had never been at the wheel of anything bigger than a saloon before going to Bosnia and some of the vehicles I found myself handling would normally have needed an HGV licence; it was only the fact that they were classified as ambulances that enabled volunteers to drive them.

The other twenty or so volunteers were all male except for a woman named Lynne Gillette. She had travelled from Manchester where she worked part-time as a temp and ran a collection point for the Appeal. Lynne was big and boisterous with dark curly hair and large brown eyes. She was twenty-six years old, about my height and wore short flared skirts and flat pumps. I liked her immediately and knew she would be good at lightening the atmosphere if things got too rough.

As I climbed into the bus I noticed that Sean had put a large photograph of Collette, an American woman with whom he had fallen in love on the last trip, right at the front so that he could look at her all the way to Bosnia where she was waiting for him. I would tease Sean unmercifully whenever I caught him gazing at her in adoration.

The journey to Split was uneventful if tiring, but I enjoyed the sensation of driving a bus. As we reached the Croatian/Bosnian border I noticed a crowd waiting at the side of the road. A young man was jumping up and down and I realised he was trying to attract my attention. It was Seemo from Posušje.

'Sally,' he called excitedly, 'Me go Italy.'

I jumped down from the bus and ran over to the group which included most of the refugees I had met two weeks before and, as fast as I could, I unloaded the supplies I had collected for particular individuals. A pale and exhausted volunteer explained what had happened. After he had returned to Posušje two drunken HVO soldiers had entered the school and beaten up some of the refugees and the volunteers who had tried to intervene. Shortly afterwards the HVO had fired into the building albeit over the heads of its inhabitants.

As a result the Italian volunteers had persuaded the Red Cross to transfer the refugees to Italy. Most, like Seemo, were thrilled; others were tremendously sad, convinced they would never return.

He believed the attack had been a deliberate attempt to frighten them away. Seven Posušje Croats had been killed by Muslim soldiers and this was their retaliation. Now four hundred Croatian refugees, forced out of their homes in Central Bosnia, would be moving into the school. Whatever the causes I was glad that these people would finally be safe. I gave Seemo some clothes and toiletries and Mama a new navy skirt, white blouse and beautiful hand crocheted shawl. For the young women I had boxes of cosmetics and perfumes, things they had not seen for a long time, frivolous perhaps but essential for morale. We kissed and hugged at the roadside while the Croatian police signalled angrily to me to move on.

During the next couple of days in Medugorje both Lynne and I grew increasingly unhappy with the situation. As the conflict escalated the Croats seemed less and less willing to let the Muslims have their share of the aid. We were told for instance that we would not be allowed to take supplies to the Muslim camp of Čapljina a mere half hour's drive away and that all the vehicles must be handed over to the Catholic priests. It was only our angry insistence that eventually persuaded them otherwise.

When we had finally emptied our vehicles I suggested we take the children to a nearby waterfall for a picnic. It was their first outing in nearly a year and their faces were constantly beaming as they splashed through the water and ate from an improvised barbecue. The mothers who had hardly left the camp for months either enjoyed the break as much as the children. All the way home we sang songs in English and Serbo-Croat.

Sean and Collette were inseparable and seemed more in love each day. Collette introduced me to 'the Boys', a group of mercenaries, though they preferred to be called foreign nationals since, they said, they fought not for financial gain which was negligible but to defend the Croats and Muslims against the Serbs.

They were a curious mixture: Thierry, a charming Frenchman and ex-Legionnaire who had fought previously with the Armijh (the joint Muslim/Croatian force); Paddy, a 23-year-old Irishman with an infectious smile; Dave, ex-British army, short, broad and extremely tough. Others included a Dutchman and a pot-smoking Croatian hippy. The squad was called *Grdani* or The Ugly Ones in English.

I found myself intrigued by them. At one level they seemed so ordinary – laughing, joking, flirting, talking of their homes – yet I knew that Thierry, who detested cruelty to women, children or old people, was none the less a sniper who could pick off his victims with deadly accuracy and that each of his fellows was equally ready to kill in cold-blood.

After her visit to Čapljina Lynne decided that she now wanted to do more than simply collect aid. Although she had done a brilliant job of gathering and sorting literally tons of stuff over the past months in Britain, she had come to the conclusion that the convoys were now too biased. I felt the same way: although we had managed to deliver to Muslim camps it would soon become dangerous, even impossible.

She thought she would like to work as a hands-on volunteer instead, possibly in Čapljina. I had learned that there was still a small Jewish community somewhere in West Mostar and I wanted to help them on my next visit. I felt it would be easier to direct my efforts towards a small neutral group rather than choose one side or the other. I had little idea what form my help should take or even how I would be able to afford to return but I was determined to find a way. Bosnia, a place I had hardly heard of before the conflict, and its people had got under my skin.

My third trip was with the International Women's Convoy

which consisted of nearly forty women, half British and half American, in ten vehicles. Some were pilgrims, others nurses, teachers, housewives and mothers. Three were Jewish and going for the same reasons as myself.

The journey this time was really interesting. The women bonded quickly and the atmosphere was full of expectation, excitement and, since this was the first trip to a war zone for most of them, more than a little fear. Because it was a women's convoy we were warned there might be trouble; in fact the women were much less inclined to whinge and complain than any of the men I had travelled with, even when we broke down in foul weather at the top of Mont Blanc.

Although most of the aid was again unloaded into the Medugorje warehouse I had managed to warn some of the women that supplies were needed just as badly elsewhere and four American women had given me their medical equipment to distribute as I thought best.

We arranged another trip for the women and children of the Pax Hotel and as I was driving back at the end of the day I suddenly recognised my name being sung. One of the mothers had said the children had made the song up themselves and that it went something like 'our Sally accelerates and no one can overtake her.' In truth I was driving quite slowly because I had so many passengers but every now and then I would switch on the siren and the blue light on top of the old Bedford ambulance I was driving which must have given the children the impression we were speeding along for they screamed in delight. I felt honoured by 'my song' and very moved by another they sang, the song of Pax or song of peace. Indeed there were few of us who did not finish the journey with a lump in the throat.

Lynne arrived next day and we decided to move into the

hotel in Čitluk where Collette and the Boys were staying. It was cheap and not too far from Mostar. I imagined Lynne would stay there until she could get a position at Čapljina. However that area was suddenly declared out of bounds to aid workers so she decided to stay and help me.

I managed to arrange a meeting at a hospital on the outskirts of Mostar with a Dr Vladlena Atijus, an anaesthetist on loan from Zagreb who was herself Jewish and able to give me a great deal of information about the community I was seeking. Vladlena, a big busty woman in her late forties, had only just arrived in Mostar but was already taking charge. Everyone seemed to like her loud, no-nonsense approach.

She spoke to me between operations. Young men were being brought in to have bullets or shrapnel removed. One died while I was there. Vladlena came back into the staff room where I was waiting. She was flushed and tears were running down her full cheeks. 'You see what they do to us,' she cried, 'these Muslims whom you in the West so pity. They kill us, our parents, our husbands, our children. Come.'

She led me by the hand through wards filled with the scarred and bandaged victims of the war raging less than two kilometres away in the centre of the city. I promised to bring her the medical supplies I had been given.

As I was driven back in the army vehicle she had arranged, I thought about what she had told me of the Jewish community. Some had gone to Israel at the outbreak of war, but around seventy remained, mainly elderly people who refused to leave their homes despite the fact that many were on or near the front line in West Mostar. Only five Jews were still in East Mostar and no one had heard from them for three months.

One of the community leaders was a man called Zoran, a

respected engineer who had helped build many of the bridges which were now being systematically destroyed. The Jews were considered neutral by both Croats and Muslims and respected by both sides.

The Čitluk Hotel was dark and dingy and our tiny room had space only for two lumpy single beds, a shower and a toilet. The water came on for two hours a day, and always at different times, but at least the accommodation cost only two hundred German marks a month, a major consideration since neither Lynne nor I had much money. Indeed I had had to sell the only piece of jewellery I owned of any value for a few hundred pounds to finance my return.

It was also an unofficial military hotel, housing *Grdani* soldiers and doctors who had been given military status at the outbreak of war. It was very disconcerting to be surrounded by men in uniform at meal times but the hotel had the only restaurant in town: the rest were without electricity.

Collette and Sean lived on the floor below us and we spent a lot of time together. Collette was twenty-seven, extrovert and amusing and extremely popular with the residents, especially 'the Boys' who shared two rooms down the hall. She could strip down a gun faster than most of them, was a crack shot and played a mean hand of cards. She was small and attractive with startling green eyes, and a habit of crying, 'ohmygad' when surprised.

Yet she was a peacenik by conviction who wanted nothing more than an end to the war. Originally from Michigan, she had come over to work in the Muslim refugee camps and then for a local aid agency. Now she helped transport seriously wounded patients from the West Mostar hospital to Split where facilities were better.

47

Sean who had been with the British territorial army was training to join *Grdani*. He had a uniform and a rifle but was waiting for a permit to fight. Lynne and I spent many hours trying to talk him out of it but he was convinced that any experience alongside the Boys would make astonishing pictures. He and Collette made an odd couple: he over six feet tall in his camouflage and Doc Martens with a Kalashnikov across his shoulder; she a 5ft 2ins sun-streaked blonde in surgical greens.

We had been at the hotel only a couple of days when Zoran sent a young boy to look for me. Damir Rozic was only sixteen but he had hitch-hiked through a highly dangerous area to find me. I borrowed a one ton armour-plated ambulance from the Boys and set off with Damir and Lynne for the front line hospital in West Mostar where his mother Erna met us.

Her father had been in the front line hospital for three months and was suffering from terrible bed sores because there was no rubbing alcohol. He was also in desperate need of a particular antibiotic which was no longer obtainable in the city. Without it, said Erna, her beautiful eyes filling with tears, he would die. I was shocked, knowing how much medical aid was pouring into Bosnia, to find a man dying for lack of it. Where was everything going?

Erna, who dodged sniper fire every day to visit her father, took us into the hospital. It was pockmarked with bullet and shrapnel holes and the only glass left was in jagged shards around the windows. The wards had all been moved to the basement – above ground was too dangerous – and as we went in I was hit by the overpowering smell in the airless rooms.

We passed rows of patients, each face seeming in the pale light more haunted than the one before, until we reached the bed of Damir's grandfather. His eyes were huge in his gaunt face and his skin seemed stretched to breaking point over his cheek bones. As Erna bent to kiss him I saw him wince at even that slight pressure on his weathered face.

He indicated that he wanted a cigarette and I handed over a carton I had brought with me. His eyes swivelled towards me as he spoke to Erna in a voice rough and cracking. As she explained who I was he looked me up and down and half smiled. His thin leg was propped up on a pillow, a metal pin holding the festering wound together.

Damir told me what had happened. His grandfather who was eighty-four and deaf had been walking outside his apartment three months before when an attack began. The old man failed to hear the shots and was struck in the leg by a phosphorus tracer bullet. He had managed to roll beneath a car and lay there in agony for seven hours before he was found by the HVO police.

Appalled by the story I told Damir to assure his mother and grandfather that I would return as soon as possible with the appropriate antibiotic. As we drove home Damir told me his grandmother had not been able to see her husband because she was crippled with arthritis and barely able to walk. Instead she remained in her apartment day and night, the windows boarded up to protect her from both the elements and the continuous small-arms fire.

Damir's home was on the third floor of a badly damaged building only fifty metres from the front line. Thirty shells had landed there during the past two years and their own balcony door had been blown off in one attack. Yet the apartment was clean and tidy and nicely furnished though they dared not switch on their lights in the rooms which faced the east side. The boy had long since moved out of his own room which looked that way into his mother's.

We sat around a large coffee table and drank squash for there was no coffee; it was too expensive to buy on the black market. Damir's shorts were old and worn, not through fashion as they might have been elsewhere, but through necessity: they had been unable to buy him any new ones since the war began.

Their dog jumped on to my lap. They had a cat too but it spent most of its time hiding in the bathroom, terrified by the bangs outside. The dog was a war puppy and had grown up with the noise but the cat remained in an almost constant state of terror, poor thing. The sheer ordinary homeliness of the place only served to reinforce my sense of the bizarre. We were sitting chatting in a nice neat room while every few minutes outside there would be a burst of machine-gun fire or the loud pop-pop-pop of sniper rifles. Now and then I would jump as a shell landed but Damir and his mother hardly seemed to notice.

There was a knock at the door and a man in his late fifties with a broad smile and ruddy cheeks entered. He was sweating profusely and his shirt was stained across his chest. As he mopped his forehead and shook my hand so hard it almost hurt Damir introduced him: 'Zoran, president of the Jewish community.'

Speaking in German which both Lynne and I understood he described his people's plight. He interspersed his conversation with prods and thumps to emphasise his words, almost bruising those beside him in the process. Although more than a hundred packages had been sent out the previous September only half had arrived and since then there had been nothing. Each family had fifty German marks a month, which was not enough to provide the basics, let alone fresh fruit or vegetables.

Most of those who had stayed behind were elderly and many

were suffering badly from their nerves. Some were diabetic too and it was virtually impossible to get either insulin or sedatives to help them sleep. The aid warehouse which was run from an old woman's front room was empty now except for two sprouting potatoes lying on the floor. I promised him I would do all I could to get more aid and we said goodbye. Damir guided us to the Čitluk road before making his way back on foot through the dangerous streets.

Back at the hotel Lynne faxed as many aid agencies as she could but only one replied, a German organisation based in Zagreb, who assured her a doctor would drive down with medical supplies. Meanwhile I visited Albert Benabou, the UN's civil affairs officer at the base in Medugorje and requested help. An Israeli himself, Albert was surprised at the number of Jews remaining. I gave him a list of names with crosses against those who wished to leave and he allowed me to use his phone to call a major Jewish charity in Britain.

Despite my insistence to the contrary they were convinced that there was still a full warehouse in Split, a conviction repeated in a phone call to me at the hotel from one of their officials later that night. Eventually the exchange became heated. I had just packed a suitcase, she suggested, and arrived in Bosnia with no foreknowledge or experience. I tried to point out that this was irrelevant anyway but she seemed to have no interest in listening to me.

'We are responsible for aid to Bosnia and do not need your help. I'm sure you mean well but your information is completely wrong. Aid goes out every month and Zoran knows he can collect whatever he wants from our warehouse in Split.'

'He tried that once and was turned away empty-handed,' I said, 'and anyway he doesn't have transport. All cars were commandeered by the army.'

'I suggest you go home,' she said and hung up.

I repeated the conversation to Lynne who was as surprised as I was. It seemed that nobody cared what we were trying to do and we felt extremely frustrated. It was as if we were banging our heads against a brick wall. As time went by, however, we were to find that such attitudes were almost an inherent part of large organisations. They had their own established way of doing things and they did not want an outsider rocking the boat. Strangled by bureaucracy, they seemed incapable of swift and decisive action in emergencies. Everything had to be done through the 'proper channels' regardless of the desperation of those in need.

It was in fact to be three months before any aid reached Zoran's community and that was only after I wrote to Michael Mendoza, a presenter on Spectrum, the Jewish radio station in London. He not only made my plea for help public, he continued to support and defend my actions as I advanced ever deeper into the chaos that was Bosnia.

5

THE BABY BRIGADIER

On our next visit to the Bielje Brig hospital Lynne and I were introduced to many of the staff. One of the doctors had heard that I was trying to rent a car and offered me his own Renault Four. We agreed on a rate of a hundred marks a week, gave him two hundred then and there and took the keys. I asked Vladlena if it would be possible to get a paper proving my legal right to drive the car. She beamed and marched off down the corridor, returning a few moments later with a tall, dark-skinned man in uniform.

'Dr Ivan Bagaric,' she announced proudly. Ivan Bagaric was a handsome man with dark glittering eyes and thick black wavy hair. We shook hands and I felt my own enveloped in his. It was large and warm and gripped mine just a little longer than necessary.

He spoke no English but Vladlena translated in a mixture of German and broken English. He grinned with pleasure when she told him I was Jewish which surprised me: I thought Croats were anti-semitic since they had been Hitler's allies in the Second World War.

But Dr Bagaric spoke of his admiration for Vladlena and his

affection for Zoran and offered his help immediately I told him about the problems there. He would, he said, arrange for Zoran to get whatever he needed from the priests at Medugorje. I also told him about Damir's grandfather and he assured me he would try to get him transferred to this hospital which was far better equipped and much safer.

He would have a document prepared for me on HVO notepaper, stamped by the Ministry of Defence and signed by him, which would allow me to pass back and forth through Croat checkpoints anywhere in Herzegovina. We asked him about the safety of travelling alone through West Mostar and he suggested I carry his revolver.

I was shocked. I was after all a foreigner and a stranger to him. But he was serious. I told him I had no experience with firearms but he explained that the most important aspect of the revolver was that it belonged to him. It was a .38 special, extremely rare in the city, and therefore recognisable as his and a deterrent to any trigger-happy soldier.

As I considered the gun I recalled an incident that had happened on my second trip to Bosnia. Sean and I were on our way back from West Mostar with a minibus full of pilgrims when I saw a large red fire truck flashing at me in my mirror.

I thought it wanted to overtake but we were on a narrow ridge and there was no room. As I took a bend I saw a gap and pulled in but instead of passing us the truck pulled alongside, blocking the road. Two soldiers jumped out and pointed their machine-guns at us. I had never been on the wrong end of a gun barrel before but I remained strangely calm as did Sean while the others began to panic.

The soldiers wanted our cameras. One man had a small

camcorder and begged them not to take it, however when a soldier cocked his weapon the cameras were swiftly handed over.

To our astonishment we got them back a few days later. We had recounted our story at the hotel and obviously pressure had been brought to bear on the bandit soldiers. But the experience taught me that this was a lawless area. Many troops were undisciplined and some little better than marauding gangs. I would accept Ivan's offer of his pistol.

The gun was unloaded as ammunition for this type of weapon was scarce and I assured him I would be happier if it remained that way. He shook his dark head vehemently.

'An unloaded gun is far more dangerous than a loaded one,' he said. 'Never point a weapon at a man unless you are prepared to use it.'

He handed me the small brown revolver and said he would give me the bullets at the Čitluk Hotel where he stayed during the week.

Lynne, who was to run the administrative side of our operative while I did the visits and deliveries, was very unhappy about the gun. She believed it was wrong for aid workers to be armed and although I agreed with her in principle I also knew that if I was to travel around on my own it could be a life-saver. By the time we left Mostar shortly before the six o'clock curfew we had acquired a car, a weapon and the correct documentation: we could begin the next day.

I have wondered many times since about the strange chemistry between myself and Ivan Bagaric and why he should go out of his way to help a stranger.

Perhaps there was a spark at that first fateful meeting, perhaps he knew instinctively that here was someone he could trust, perhaps he was even attracted to me. Certainly as time passed I came to know that he liked me. He seemed impressed by the fact that I was Jewish: I think he identified very strongly with the Jews' struggle for a homeland. He was fascinated by Israel, partly because it was the Holy Land for him too and partly because he admired the way the Israelis did things: their fighting forces, their discipline, the organisation of their army field hospitals. It was his dream to set foot there.

I think he was also intrigued by the idea of a woman in a war zone. He had a traditional, even old-fashioned, attitude towards women and yet he had a sneaking admiration for one who was doing what he would have thought of as 'man's work'.

He liked too the fact that I would stand my ground in an argument with him. If he had known the phrase he would probably have said I had a 'bit of bottle'.

For my part I liked and admired him enormously but I was never romantically inclined towards him. He was a curious mixture of the bear-like and the boyish. He was only the same age as me which is why I nicknamed him the 'baby brigadier': I had always imagined brigadiers to be grey-haired old men.

My first trip was to the Rozics' apartment where I would stay the weekend. Damir helped me carry in a couple of large boxes of items that I had managed to find at a small grocer's in Čitluk and I watched with great satisfaction as Erna, eyes wide with delight, filled up her empty shelves with all those everyday items which had been unavailable for so long.

She also took pleasure in sharing part of the precious load with her neighbours. Some were Muslims who were trying desperately to keep a low profile in the hope of avoiding eviction or arrest but Erna and her family were without racial or religious discrimination. Indeed her husband Stipe, who worked for the police administration department, had helped many obtain visas and other documentation.

Zoran came to visit, sweating as usual, and announced he would take me to his office on the front line in the morning. That evening Erna cooked a wonderful meal which tasted particularly delicious after the greasy fried food at the Čitluk Hotel. It was lovely to see that family eating well for the first time in months. They were all undernourished. Damir was a gangly teenager anyway but his mother was so thin her shoulder blades stuck out and her clothes hung off her. Even Stipe seemed lost in his sweater. I had shed a few kilos since I arrived in Bosnia but compared to them I felt overweight.

Suddenly there was a loud explosion right above us. I wanted to dive under the table but no one else moved; they just carried on eating. We learned later that four rocket-propelled grenades had landed on the apartment block roof although fortunately no one had been hurt.

The electricity came on for a couple of hours that night and we were able to watch clips from Sky and CNN of Operation Irma, the airlift of wounded people from Sarajevo which had been inspired by the plight of one desperately ill little girl.

But the newsreel made Stipe angry. It was, he said, just a publicity stunt for political gain. 'Why Sarajevo?' he asked. 'Sarajevo was in a terrible state for a long time and the world knew it. But aid is reaching the people now, they have water and electricity. They also have the media.

'But what about Mostar? Nobody knows or cares about Mostar. This remarkable city is dying and no one is doing anything. Why?'

I could not answer him. Although it was heartening to see some people being flown out of Sarajevo I was saddened at the thought of all those left behind, especially the children. And I thought about similar horrors just a few streets away in East Mostar, all those who were sick and starving and dying because no one could get in or out. I could hardly bear to imagine the condition of a place which had seen no aid for months, whose inhabitants were being shelled and shot at far more intensely than anyone on this side of the line.

That night I lay listening to the soldiers in the street below. Their voices drifting through the open window mingled with the bursts of machine-gun fire and the loud thump of shells. On my way to the bathroom I found Damir staring through the kitchen window at the hills of East Mostar.

I joined him and we stared into the darkness together. He stopped me thoughtlessly lighting a cigarette which could have drawn sniper fire on either of us. I studied his profile as he watched the tracers trailing through the sky and shuddered not from cold but from fear that a boy could find all this so normal.

Here was someone who had witnessed two years of war on his doorstep. He had seen his school destroyed by Serbian shells, seen his friends injured, even killed. He had held his mother while she cried in fear for her mother and her father. He had no social life, no studies, no discos or coffee bars to go to, no sports to play, in fact none of the pleasures we take for granted.

For him life meant only the odd snatched conversation on an empty rubble-strewn street with friends who hardly flinched as a shell exploded nearby; the terrifying dashes across the main junctions to avoid sniper fire; the anxious wait for his mother to return from her visits to the hospital; and the terrible fear that the war would go on and on and soon he too would be called to fight and ordered to kill those who had once been his neighbours.

If ever a teenager could be forgiven for getting in with a bad crowd, for escaping into drugs or crime it was him. But he did none of these things. Instead he risked his life delivering messages because no one had cars or telephones. He helped his parents by keeping their spirits up and taught himself English from the odd snippets on TV.

I felt proud to know him and as I watched his face in the flickering light I swore to myself that I would get him away from this nightmare. That was what his parents wanted more than anything. Erna could not leave her sick elderly parents or the man she loved but she wanted her son to be safe, able to live some kind of normal life.

Zoran arrived on time the next morning and I was surprised when Erna hugged me closely. She was not a particularly demonstrative person but she was aware that the Hotel Era where Zoran had his office was in a very dangerous part of the city. 'Take care of her,' she called to him as we drove away.

In the kitchen that morning she had told me that they loved having me around because I was a breath of fresh air in their lives and I gave them hope. I had never felt so needed but I also felt the terrible burden of responsibility.

Zoran directed me over a crossroad which separated east from west. An overturned truck was the only defence from ground attacks and as we passed I could hear the loud crack of rifle fire aimed at the car. I weaved the small Renault through the streets until we reached a large blackened building which was the Hotel Era. We parked quickly and dashed inside past several HVO soldiers lounging in the doorway.

He told me that this building, originally a rest home for the elderly, housed those who did not want to leave and others who had nowhere else to go. There were many elderly refugees too: Serbs, Muslims, Jews and Croats all living peacefully together in contrast to those outside. The building was also used as HVO headquarters and was therefore a target. It had been badly damaged by constant bombardment; most of the windows were shattered and glass littered the floor.

As we walked down the corridors we had to crouch low to avoid being targets ourselves. I glanced out across the street, appalled to see once beautiful buildings now charred and pockmarked with bullet holes or missing their top floors where shells had hit the roof. Above it all was the clear blue sky and sunlight glinted on the broken glass.

People shuffled past us. Some muttered a greeting, others ignored us and stared blankly ahead, lost in their own thoughts. All of them were old enough to have been through the Second World War and to have survived the atrocities which the world had vowed must never be repeated. And I wondered what they thought of all the bloodshed and cruelty and slaughter happening over again just beyond the door.

Zoran's office was situated at the front of the building facing the east side of the city but on a corner which meant the window area was relatively safe provided one did not peer over the ledge. Shelves were piled high with books many of them about Mostar, many about Israel where Zoran's wife and children now were. A large picture of Tito dominated the room.

He offered me a glass of schnapps but it was too early for alcohol and anyway I wanted to keep a clear head in such surroundings. We were much closer to the fighting here and the sounds of war were much louder. I jumped every time a shell exploded outside but, like so many others I had seen, Zoran appeared not even to notice.

We spent an hour in the tiny room as he told me the history of his people and the city of which he was so proud. Afterwards we went downstairs to the basement where two old women were living beneath the staircase. One of them had had a room upstairs and had stayed on when the fighting began but the room had been destroyed in an explosion a few days earlier and everything she owned had been lost. I offered to bring her some things but she said she no longer needed anything. The other woman was a refugee from the east. She had lost her home and her family had been separated in the confusion. She wept constantly and flinched at every sound.

Later that day Zoran took me to an apartment building not far from the main road. As we climbed to a top floor he warned me not to mention what I was about to see to anyone. As we knocked at the door and waited I could hear sounds of panicky movements coming from the other side and a nervous-looking woman of about forty finally opened the door.

The fear in her eyes disappeared as she recognised Zoran and she ushered us quickly inside. In the sitting room two more women, one in her seventies and the other in her early thirties, were sitting on the couch beside a boy of seven or eight.

The woman who had opened the door introduced herself. Until recently she had been a Croatian high court judge but had been forced to resign because she was married to a Muslim. Her husband had escaped to Austria and she was to join him shortly, leaving behind her attractive book-filled apartment and most of her belongings. The older woman was her mother-in-law and the younger her sister-in-law.

We drank coffee as she and Zoran conversed in their own language, occasionally glancing across at me. Finally they decided to trust me. The old lady's son, they revealed, the husband of the younger woman, was still living in the apartment, hidden in a cupboard in the hall. Every knock at the door threw them into a panic, as they expected he might be discovered and betrayed to the authorities at any time. The little boy was his son. As I listened I was reminded of *The Diary of Anne Frank* and wondered yet again how history could be repeating itself in this appalling way.

The reason for our visit now became clear. This man had worked alongside Zoran as an engineer for many years and was desperate for a visa to another country. Even with such a document he would still have to be smuggled into Croatia since as a man he was listed for internment. What the family wanted me to do was take his mother across the border into Croatia where her other two sons were waiting with the documentation that would allow her to travel to Austria. Zoran hoped I could somehow get her across at Metkovic and drive her to Makarska in Croatia.

I pointed out that smuggling an old woman in the boot of a Renault Four would be not only irresponsible but dangerous in the dreadful heat. But I assured them I would try to do something, though as yet I did not know exactly what. Before I left the man came out to meet me, looking pale and drawn from his months in hiding. He clasped my hand warmly and thanked me in advance for helping his mother.

The next day I went to see Ivan Bagaric and asked tentatively for his advice. I gave him no names saying only that I knew an old Muslim woman who wanted to leave the country. He said visas had been very hard to obtain because thousands of refugees, mainly the old and the very young, had been pouring into Croatia from Bosnia, putting an enormous extra strain on an already over-stretched country. The government therefore was now allowing in only those who had a visa for another country or those who were self-sufficient.

'Would you help me in this case?' I asked, 'she really is leaving the country.'

He looked thoughtful for a moment and then asked for the woman's name. I left his office with the transit visa for her in my pocket. He had warned me that it might not be enough and that if it were discovered she was a Muslim she could be sent back and I could find myself in a great deal of trouble. But I only had to think of that man in his twilight world and his mother forced to witness his suffering and I knew I would take the risk. I arranged a day for later that week when I would come to fetch her with Zoran who would act as translator and guide.

When the morning came I waited outside in the car while Zoran went in to collect her. I did not want to see her farewells to the loved ones she knew she may never see again. And I thought of the little boy who would have to say goodbye to his grandmother and then continue to live with his dreadful secret.

I had dressed in khaki shorts and a white T-shirt and carried a few things in a shoulder bag given to me by a soldier at the hotel. It was standard HVO issue and I hoped it would serve as a sign of my connection with the army. Inside was the gun, still unloaded, but which I dared not leave at the hotel in case it was stolen. It was worth at least a thousand marks, a year's pay for an officer.

The old woman shuffled across the street behind Zoran carrying her belongings in two small carrier bags. Tears pricked my eyes. How do you decide what possessions to take to a new country, how can you bear to leave a lifetime's worth of precious mementos behind? She climbed slowly into the car obviously reluctant to leave but Zoran hurried her, wanting to be on our way. He was worried and his normally smiling face was sombre.

We drove along Mostar's main tree-lined avenue, through deserted streets, past shelled buildings and up the mountain road to the first checkpoint. To Zoran's surprise I was not even stopped; probably the soldiers had grown used to my little Renault whizzing in and out of the city.

It took about an hour to reach Metkovic where we would cross the two checkpoints that marked the border. The tension in the car as we approached the first barrier was almost palpable but the policeman on duty barely glanced at us as he waved us through. The next barrier was manned by the Croatian police and it was the one where I had been warned to expect more trouble. As we pulled up I could feel Zoran tensing beside me in the passenger seat and I glanced in the mirror at the old woman.

'Are you all right?' I asked but she shrugged and nodded. A policeman approached and gestured for my documents. I gave him my passport and the letter Ivan had written authorising my passage through all checkpoints in Bosnia Herzegovina. To our surprise and great relief he waved us through without even looking at my passengers' papers. As I accelerated away the old woman leaned forward and squeezed my shoulder. Looking in the mirror I could see her nodding happily.

We sped along the Croatian coast to Makarska in high spirits. Zoran told me to pull up outside a seafront guest house and as I parked three big handsome men strode towards us. One of them opened the back door and with a cry of 'Mama' swept the old woman into his arms and half carried, half dragged her from her seat. They hugged and kissed and then embraced Zoran as I looked on with a glow of satisfaction.

Suddenly they descended on the car and gave me the same treatment.

The judge had arrived safely too and introduced me to her husband and brothers-in-law.

'You have given them back their mother,' she said. 'Thank you.'

The old woman took my face in her worn, wrinkled hands and kissed me, tears streaming down her face. It was the most moving kiss I had ever been given.

6

A VISIT FROM A STRANGER

Lynne was very relieved to see me on my return. Apparently one of the Boys had been told that due to my 'interference' in the delivery of aid from the Medugorje appeal – possibly due to my insistence that the Muslims had a fair share – I was to have been deported but that because I had connections with people in high places this would not now happen. I could only assume that the 'baby brigadier', Ivan Bagaric, had intervened.

That night, in Collette and Sean's room as it was the largest, we celebrated the successful evacuation. Thierry wanted his fortune told so I brought my pack of Tarot cards with me. The rest of the Boys decided to have their cards read too. Each shuffle produced similar forecasts, none of them too bad – except for Paddy's. The seventh card out which depicts the immediate future was the Ten of Swords, a card supposed to foretell disaster or violence.

I asked him what had been in his mind when he shuffled the cards and he said he had asked about a mission they were all due to go on the following day. At once I asked him not to go. We all knew he was going back to Ireland at the end of the month and it seemed only right to be safe rather than sorry.

But Paddy insisted that he must go: it was probably the last time he would fight with the boys and he was not prepared to let them down. There was nothing more I could do except hope that the cards were nothing more than meaningless bits of coloured paper.

The next evening Collette came running out to our car on our return from the Pax. She was terribly upset and warned us to be careful what we said inside the hotel. I soon understood why. Paddy, thirty-second in line as the soldiers walked in single file along a track near Gurni Vackuf had stepped on a buried mine. The explosion had torn off one leg beneath the knee and thrown him sideways. As he fell he hit a second mine which blasted his other leg away at the thigh. But he had survived and was now in hospital in Split undergoing emergency surgery.

Inside the Čitluk Hotel Thierry and the others were sitting around a table in the dining room, mute with sadness and shock. Paddy was very special to all of us. He was kind and generous and had a wonderful sense of humour. What made it even worse was that he was not even a proper soldier. He had joined the group in search of adventure and had not even told his mother where he was going.

The next day Lynne and the others went to visit him but I could not bear the thought of seeing something which I knew could have been avoided. When Lynne returned however she told me how amazing he was, how resilient and accepting. I felt I would rather have died then live on with such mutilation but Paddy had even been able to crack jokes through his pain and say things like 'Well, look on the bright side. I've always hated being short, now I can have special long artificial legs made and be tall at last.'

The squad commander was making arrangements for him to be flown home once he was fit enough to travel. It was ironic when we knew he had already made the decision to leave. The tragedy brought home to all of us how fragile we were in this war-torn country, how easy it was for one's whole life to be shattered, even lost, in a split second.

One evening Ivan introduced me to his colleagues, a group of doctors who had formed a chain of army field hospitals with Bielje Brig as its main link. They indulged in much banter and teasing but it was obvious the men held Ivan in the greatest affection and respect. A devout Catholic, he had adopted his niece and nephew after their father had been killed in the fighting and brought them to live with him. Although as yet unmarried he was devoted to his 'little family' and to his mother whom he visited as often as he could.

He was a skilled politician too who could see beyond the day to day crises. He also had the politician's knack of skirting around a subject before finally getting to the point.

One afternoon he showed me a fax headed Top Secret which had been sent to him and the other doctors from the 'new white' hospital called Nova Bila, near Novi Travnic in central Bosnia. Originally a Franciscan monastery, Nova Bila had been converted to deal with the thousands of sick and injured in the area.

The fax was a desperate plea for help – no aid or new staff had been able to reach the area for months – and Ivan wanted me to try to do something about it. When I asked whether the UN had been informed Ivan replied, 'They know but they do nothing. They have a base nearby but they don't care about Croats.'

It was the same criticism I had heard from Vladlena and

others and I did have some sympathy. It seemed to me that there was a media bias against his people. After a particularly brutal massacre of Croat civilians by Muslim forces, for example, a human rights organisation had called a press conference but few had attended and fewer still reported it.

I offered to take the fax to the UN base at Medugorje to try to persuade them to act. Ivan shrugged his consent but it was obvious he had no faith in them.

As I drove there I kept a close watch on my rear view mirror for although my visit was on behalf of the Croats the UN were so unpopular I feared I might be seen as one of their spies by the local soldiers, especially as I was living cheek by jowl with the Croatian military.

The entrance was manned by a couple of Spanish soldiers who watched the road from behind a pile of sandbags. I gave my name and asked for Albert Benabou but he was not in his office. Instead I was taken to meet an English-speaking officer. Having offered me coffee he asked how he could be of help.

I spoke of the problems the doctors were facing in central Bosnia and how children as well as adults were dying there through lack of medical supplies. The captain rested his chin on his hands and surveyed me coldly. What, he asked, was my interest in the matter?

'I want to see these people helped,' I said, surprised he should even wonder.

'Miss Becker, we have a base nearby in Kiseljak. We have British troops based in Vitez. I am sure Nova Bila does not need your help.'

I was tempted to shove the fax in his face, despite its Top Secret designation, so he could read it with his own eyes. Instead I said:

'I have seen a document faxed to Mostar hospital. It was not for my attention, it was for the doctors'. Nova Bila is desperate. It's the only hospital in the area and it is responsible for the health of thousands.'

He smiled, slightly condescendingly I thought. 'The Croats produce propaganda of this type all the time. Take no notice.'

I was confused. Could he be right and I was just being used?

'Could I go there on one of your convoys and make an assessment for myself?' I asked.

'We can't let you join one of our convoys. You are not authorised. Only UN personnel can ride in our vehicles. And besides, there aren't any convoys planned for that area at the moment. We use helicopters.'

'Well, could I go in a helicopter?'

The captain laughed. 'Believe me, all the Croats want is an aerial view of central Bosnia to assist their military operations.'

'Why can't I go?' I persisted. 'I'd take the aid in myself by road if I could but I've only got a Renault Four. That's hardly an armour-plated four-wheel drive is it and anyway how much aid could I fit in?'

'I've told you,' he replied. 'They don't need anything. It's propaganda. Stick to what you're doing.' And he stood up.

As I prepared to drive away from the base I spotted a UN landrover with the word UNICEF written on its side. I have always had the greatest respect for the United Nations Childrens Emergency Fund and on impulse I went over to the young woman who was just climbing into the vehicle. I told her who I was and she seemed keen for me to meet her boss, a Frenchwoman called Danielle, and led me to their apartment just along the road from the base.

There Danielle, a strikingly attractive blonde, told me about herself and her mission in life of helping children. My impression was of a sincere and honest woman and a very brave one. She and her colleague were most interested in the fact that I was able to travel freely in and around Mostar: apparently I was one of the few foreign aid workers allowed this privilege. Danielle was anxious to assess the position in Mostar's orphanages which held both Muslim and Croatian children. She was of course most concerned to reach East Mostar and would join the first convoy that was allowed in.

Suddenly, as we were discussing all the possibilities – I thought I might be able to arrange something through Ivan – she let out an ear-piercing shriek. A spider was meandering across the floor. 'Mon Dieu,' she cried. 'Get eet out, kill eet, kill eet.'

I laughed aloud. Here was this extraordinarily courageous woman, unfazed by shell and shot and bullying soldiers, reduced to a gibbering wreck at the mere sight of a spider.

Within a couple of days I had managed to persuade Ivan to let Danielle enter Mostar on an unofficial basis but then word came through that permission had finally been granted for a convoy to enter the east side. That was the chance she had been waiting for and I wished her every success.

One afternoon a curious incident occurred. Thierry invited Lynne and myself to his room to meet a man who introduced himself as a journalist. By that time I had gained some experience of the media. From an initial interview in my local paper, the *Evening Argus*, interest in me and what I was doing had snowballed to the point where it seemed every newspaper, radio station and TV channel wanted an interview.

Until then the world's press had been focused on Sarajevo: Mostar was the forgotten city. But when it emerged that a

British woman was actually able to give a first-hand account of the conditions there the phone never stopped ringing. The fact that Sally Becker, an independent aid worker, could travel freely around a war-torn city from which the UN and other important agencies were banned was, it seemed, a great human interest story.

The Croats of course were delighted to have a 'spokesperson' to draw attention to problems which had hitherto gone unnoticed. Mostar became 'hot news' and the press began to arrive from all over the world.

So I was not surprised to be asked for yet another interview, this time, according to the newcomer, for a Danish paper. And yet there was something about this suntanned stranger with his tape recorder that aroused my suspicions. I insisted Lynne go first. She had been very much the unsung heroine in the back room and I thought it time she had her share of the limelight.

As I listened to his questions I could not shake the feeling that something was not quite right. To this day I cannot put my finger on why but ten minutes into the interview I decided to challenge him. He was not a journalist, was he, I demanded, but some sort of investigator?

He blushed furiously beneath his tan. Yes, he was an investigator of sorts, he admitted. He was a member of UNCIPOL, the UN's civil police, his name was Leo and the interview had been a device to gain insight into my character: he needed my help.

'I don't have time to explain now,' he said. 'But I'll return tonight if you don't mind. And I would like to talk to you alone.'

I shrugged. 'I'll be here,' I said, 'but I'd really like to know what this is all about. And I want Lynne to hear it too.'

As he left Lynne gave a rueful laugh. 'Isn't that typical,' she said, 'The first time someone actually wants to interview me it turns out to be a con.'

Leo returned that evening, wearing his full UNCIPOL uniform and pale blue helmet. I felt nervous when I saw him. Perhaps we were already slightly paranoid but these were tense times and we were foreigners in a hotel used by the military. To be seen meeting a UN officer could be courting trouble. Besides there was a young soldier staying down the corridor who hated the United Nations with a near-pathological intensity. He had lost his wife and child as a result, he believed, of a UN mistake and he was obsessed with vengeance.

I ushered Leo inside as fast as I could and motioned to him to sit on the couch. He came quickly to the point. There was a three-year-old Muslim boy over in East Mostar called Droce Azem who had a serious heart complaint and needed immediate surgery.

'Of course, as we all know, nobody has been in or out for many weeks, months even. But if this child is not evacuated, he will die.'

I glanced at Lynne but could not read her face. 'I'm sorry if I appear stupid,' I said, 'but what's this got to do with me?'

'You've got influence with the Croats,' he said. 'You must have, you're the only aid worker allowed in and out of Mostar. I was hoping that you could get permission for the child to be evacuated from East Mostar.'

East Mostar! I stared at him in amazement. It had to be the most dangerous place in Bosnia at that time. I stood up and excused myself for a few minutes. Ivan Bagaric and a colleague were staying in the next room and I knocked on their door. With his colleague translating I explained the situation. Would it be possible, I ventured, to have permission to evacuate a sick Muslim child from East Mostar?

Ivan began a lecture on the terrible conditions facing his people in Nova Bila hospital and other areas but I interrupted him. If he would give permission for this child to be rescued, I promised, I would do all I could to draw attention to the problems in Nova Bila. The men talked it over for ten long minutes, while I nervously waited. At last Ivan's friend translated his reply, he spoke slowly in heavily accented English.

'We Croats have nothing against the innocent civilians in this war. We will give *you* permission to travel to East Mostar to evacuate not one but all the children from the hospital there. And their mothers.'

'Me!' I exclaimed in surprise. 'What about Leo? It was his request that I ask for permission.' So great was their distrust of the UN that Ivan insisted Leo could only help with the evacuation if I was the one to carry it out.

My heart leapt. I knew that this permission marked a significant new phase in the war. If successful the evacuation would be the first in the area since fighting broke out between HVO and BIH forces. For a few moments I was speechless, then 'Thank you, thank you very much,' I managed to stammer out, 'I'll go and tell him.'

Bursting with excitement I rushed to give Leo and Lynne the news. Leo was astonished to hear I had got agreement to bring out not only Droce Azem but the other children as well.

'I must of course come with you,' he stated.

'I assume we'll have some kind of armoured vehicle and an UNPROFOR (the United Nations Protection Force) escort,' I said.

'Oh, I don't think that's such a good idea,' Leo said. 'I'd

rather UNPROFOR weren't involved. UNCIPOL do a much better job but they never get any recognition.'

I stared at him with incredulity. 'You surely wouldn't want us to drive across a front line with no protection? The least we'll need is an escort in case we come under fire.'

'The Croats will arrange a ceasefire so we should be OK and I'll see what I can arrange with my own people as regards an escort.' He looked as though he wanted to be off. 'It would be helpful if you could inform the media of our intentions. The more involved they are, the more likely we are to get the support we need,' he said.

After he had gone I pondered the strangeness of the situation. The truth was I would have taken the risk to help even one child but to be given the chance to evacuate them all really defined my raison d'être.

7

HANDOUTS AND HOLDUPS

That same night I rang the BBC. We had heard that its correspondent Jeremy Bowen had got into East Mostar by trekking through the mountains on the far side. I reckoned that if the BIH could be warned of my arrival they could arrange the ceasefire and prepare the patients. I also called Sky because I knew Croatian TV carried clips from their news each night.

The following day, however, Leo arrived and told me that he would now be going to East Mostar with a convoy that had been given permission to go in. An evacuation would not be part of it but he would use the trip to make all the necessary arrangements. I could not see the sense in this: why could I not simply join the convoy and bring out the children under its protection?

I rang the UN base directly and found myself speaking to the same captain who had been so dismissive about Nova Bila. He was no more helpful this time. It was too late for me to be added to their list, he said, and no, I could not have any armoured escorts for my own mission. At least give me an armoured ambulance, I begged, but again the answer was no. If I had permission and therefore a ceasefire, he argued, I need not fear an attack.

I was appalled by his response. The United Nations had billions of dollars in funding, thousands of soldiers and hundreds of vehicles. Yet they would not lift a finger to help the rescue of wounded children from an area that had been under siege for months. It was my first real experience of UN intransigence but it was not to be my last.

I had another major problem. We were almost out of funds. The last convoy from Medugorje had nothing for us apart from a few boxes of surgical gowns and nurses' uniforms. A couple of women from the charity Haven whom we had met on the International Women's Convoy had promised funds and a vehicle but none had appeared. There was similarly no sign of the promised aid for the Jewish community. Our own money was virtually gone. If we could not pay for our base and the car we would have to go home. My family would have sent money gladly but there were no banks open to transfer the currency. The prospect of leaving with our work unfinished was heart-breaking.

We knew some Haven people were in Medugorje so we decided to go back there to see what was going on. On arrival I found Haven's press officer who was in the middle of a photo session with a little asthmatic boy for whom she had brought nebulisers. After that she spent a couple of hours taping children singing the Pax peace song for her local radio station. Eventually I managed to get to her. She had a thousand pounds which had been raised for Bosnia but one of the priests was going to take charge of it.

Could she, I pleaded, help us in any way? I told her of the planned mission, the Jewish community's needs and our own personal financial crisis. She refused abruptly and suggested it would be better to leave our work to the official organisations.

We were in despair: yet again we were up against an unbending bureaucracy. But, as I was to find again and again, just when it seems there is no way forward a path will open up from the most unlikely source.

Another woman from Haven who did have faith in us took us to meet a gentle, unassuming man called Peter Kates who had come to Medugorje as a pilgrim with his wife and daughter. Peter was a Catholic convert but he had been born a Jew and had relatives in an aid organisation in Britain whom he thought might be able to help. His daughter who had been listening to our conversation suddenly broke in: we could have the savings she had brought with her. That would not be necessary said her father. He would give us the money himself.

We had calculated that we needed a minimum of four hundred pounds to survive until our families could send someone over with more cash and that is what Peter Kates gave us. I assured him my mother would repay him as soon as he returned to England but he gestured that there was no rush. He was not a rich man, he had paid for his pilgrimage, and that of two other people who could not otherwise have afforded it, out of his savings. And yet he was prepared to believe in and trust a total stranger. I returned to Čitluk with my faith in human nature restored.

Back at the hotel I found an Independent Television News crew waiting. They wanted to film me doing a delivery to West Mostar and it seemed a good opportunity to highlight the problems there. The next day they followed Lynne and I into the city to Bielje Brig hospital and filmed me handing over the few packages I had managed to obtain. Sean and a British soldier working for the Croatian army came along as escort. They were in uniform and carried guns which I hoped would protect the crew. The media were not popular and this team were the first to be allowed through in months and now only because they were with me. The crew particularly loved filming the way I was waved through checkpoints so easily.

We picked up Damir and his mother and took them to the front line hospital to visit grandfather. The TV lights blazed down on the poor old man and the other helpless patients. I knew it was necessary but it seemed so callous and I felt terribly upset by the whole business.

The reporter also interviewed a surgeon who spoke of the hospital's policy of treating all patients equally. The war ceased for them as soon as they crossed its threshold, whether they were Muslims, Croats or Serbs. One young Muslim had been shot in the leg by a sniper from his own side while being forced to build fortifications for the HVO. It was common practice for all sides to use prisoners for dangerous jobs but I was surprised and pleased that the Croats were allowing him to discuss it with the press.

On our way out of the city I went to pay the hire fee for the Renault but found its owner had disappeared. The doctor, a Muslim, had fled with his wife and children during a weekend leave. Either he was afraid or he could no longer cope with working with the enemy. Whatever the reason he had used our two hundred marks to escape. I had become the proud owner of a Renault Four.

That night ITN called me the Angel of Mostar, repeating a phrase originally used by Sky who had picked it up from someone I had helped. With my black spiky hair I was an unlikely looking angel but the name stuck and different versions were developed as time went by: Angel of Mercy, Bosnian Angel, even Mother Theresa in Blue Jeans in Israel's most popular paper. I was amused and touched though I felt it was undeserved – I was hardly an angelic person.

The news did not include any mention of Lynne which saddened me because she had been such a tower of strength over the past two months: practical, sympathetic and always supportive even in the darkest moments. While I was dashing around the place she would beaver away back at the Čitluk Hotel, not only struggling to do the job but also to deal with the odd characters who hung around the place.

There was a particularly strange man called Eddo who used to hassle her while I was away. He was German and the worst kind of mercenary who had joined up for the sheer pleasure of killing. He was tall and skinny with long stringy fair hair and no teeth. He always carried a knife as well as two guns and he was invariably drunk which made him even more frightening.

Lynne and I had first met him when he lurched over to our table at dinner one night and began spouting insults against Muslims, interspersed with vile descriptions of how he had killed them. We were disgusted but dare not get up to leave for fear of provoking him further. Eventually he got round to the subject of Jews and how Hitler had been right, they should all have died in the gas chambers.

As he stared at me with his cold blue eyes he drew his knife and ran his finger slowly up and down the long thin blade. It glinted menacingly as he described in detail what he used it for.

I met his gaze. 'I'm Jewish, by the way,' I said. 'What'll you do? Kill me?'

He looked stunned and began to stutter. 'But you can't be, you're too nice, too attractive. Anyway I've got nothing against Jews so long as they stay in Israel.'

I could stand it no longer. I stood up and said we had work

to do. To me Eddo was an ignorant fool but he had really unnerved Lynne and it did not help that his room was next door but one to ours.

Later Ivan turned up at the hotel with bullets for the gun he had loaned me some weeks before. They were very long and pointed.

'They wouldn't definitely kill anyone, would they?' I asked nervously.

He laughed when someone translated. 'Of course they would,' he replied.

'Then I don't want them,' I said emphatically. 'I would only use a gun in self-defence to wound an attacker.'

'Then there is no point in your having the revolver,' he said and I handed it back. It meant of course that we were now defenceless. Our only weapon was a small canister of tear gas I had persuaded one of the Boys to give me. It was little enough but it made Lynne feel slightly safer with the likes of Eddo around.

The convoy that was to go into East Mostar was finally assembled on August 25. Nineteen aid-filled trucks and their UN escort were lined up in Medugorje. As they waited in the midday sun Lynne went from person to person begging for me to be allowed to join them but no one would agree.

Eventually she gave up and returned to Čitluk where I was awaiting my documentation from the local HVO general. When it finally arrived I drove out to the convoy myself hoping that the document would provoke a change of heart. I did not want to wait for Leo to return: I was afraid that any delay could jeopardise my mission and this convoy had not even set off yet. At the same time I could not risk the journey alone with no idea of the route, no guarantee of safety on the other side and only a small car in which to evacuate the sick.

By this time the convoy had reached Čitluk where it had been stopped by a group of refugees from a nearby camp. As they waited I ran past the line of trucks, searching for Leo. Finally I spotted him sitting on top of an armoured personnel carrier. I waved my document at him.

'What should I do?' I shouted.

'Just wait 'til I get back,' he called down.

I threw up my hands and returned to the hotel. The convoy stayed where it was, surrounded by a menacing crowd of refugees and local people. They were angry because they felt forgotten. All the reports to the world outside had been focusing on the Muslims: the terrible conditions they lived in, the atrocities perpetrated upon them.

But these people too had lost their homes and their loved ones; they too had been driven from their villages with nothing but the clothes they wore; they too were suffering shortages of food and other essentials. Their plight might not have been as bad as those under siege but they wanted something for themselves. Eventually the UN agreed to make a separate delivery.

A deal was also struck whereby both sides could exchange their dead. One of the awful aspects of the war was the number of bodies, civilian and military, which had to be left where they fell, sometimes for weeks, until arrangements for an exchange could be agreed and the dead laid to rest among their own kind.

Just before the convoy was due to set off a colleague of Ivan's came over to me. At least one TV crew had already got into East Mostar and broadcast some horrific pictures. What would be the effect when all these other members of the media got in with the convoy and started filing their reports? They were, he said, extremely worried.

I told him that if I could arrange something in time, I too would be going in but instead of pictures I would bring back children rescued through the humane gesture of the Croatian doctors. Surely that would serve to offset those shocking images.

'In that case,' he said, lowering his voice, 'it may be a good idea if we keep the convoy until they agree you can join.'

I was shocked to think a whole convoy could be detained on my say so.

'You can't let them do that,' I said. 'The people over there are starving. Nothing can justify keeping all this aid here while you negotiate. Media attention is focused on this hold up as it is and the world will be even more against you if you don't allow the supplies through immediately.'

He passed on my words to Ivan and within half an hour the blockade of people was dispersed anad the convoy allowed to continue. I breathed a sigh of relief: the Croats had actually decided to compromise. They had however refused to allow the press to take a satellite dish which meant no pictures could be broadcast live from within East Mostar. I think they hoped to delay any bad publicity until my return when their own humane gesture would be made public.

That evening I laid out the Tarot for myself, hoping for any card which might indicate an end to the delay. I kept picturing the children in East Mostar I had seen on the news and their appalling wounds. These were the children I was waiting to rescue. I had never been so impatient in my life. The cards were good. I hoped to God they were a true reading of the near future though I knew in my heart that even if they had been bad I would still have taken the risk.

Early the next day I went into the dining room for coffee and watched the news. The convoy was trapped in East Mostar by a large group of women and children who had blocked the main street. Apparently they were hoping that the presence of foreign aid workers and UN soldiers would act as a deterrent against Croatian shelling. The members of the convoy were now faced not only with danger and discomfort – most were without food or water – but with the embarrassment of being held hostage by women and children.

Their situation of course meant that Leo would not be coming out as quickly as he had thought and I faced yet further delay. I sat and chain-smoked and fretted until Ivan appeared at reception. He had arranged the loan of an ambulance but he could not authorise my departure. Nobody wanted to take responsibility for me without a ceasefire on the other side of the front line.

All I could do was wait and I paced the lobby, one ear to the BBC World Service. Despite pressure from Geneva and other important parties the position remained unchanged. The Bosnians were very scared. The arrival of the UN had brought a lull in the fighting for the first time in months and they were terrified that as soon as it left the attacks would begin with renewed intensity.

About five o'clock, as I sat in front of an overflowing ashtray surrounded by a sea of empty coffee cups, Lynne was called to the phone. I saw her face light up and she signalled to me that it was good news. Leo had apparently called a fellow police officer in Medugorje on the UN satellite phone and informed him it was safe for me to go in: he had arranged everything with the Muslim authorities. But I had to go at once. He had told BIH command to expect me through their checkpoint at 5.30pm. Within a minute we were plunged into a frenzy of activity. The moment had arrived. I was on my way to East Mostar.

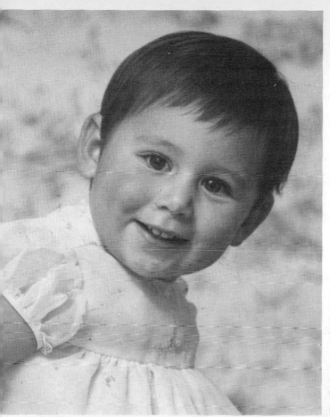

Sally as a baby. She would grow up to be 'a total tomboy'.

Sally's parents, Jack and Carol, on their wedding day with her grandparents.

Far left: Sean, taken whilst working with an HVO unit in Central Bosnia.

Collette shares a rare light moment with a refugee.

'The Boys'

Sally, Lynne and the trusty Renault 4.

The 'baby brigadier', Ivan Bagaric, wishing Sally luck before she sets off on her first mission to East Mostar.

Right: Sally takes in the appalling conditions at the Muslim hospital in East Mostar shortly before her second evacuation of injured children.

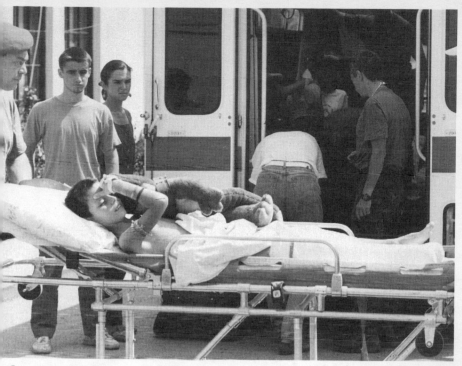

One of the children evacuated by Sally during her first mission to East Mostar is carried out of her ambulance by UN soldiers. The UN were not to be so obliging on the next mission.

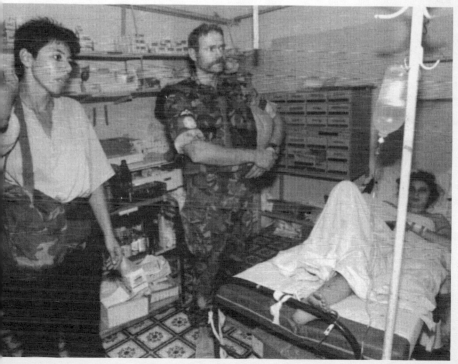

Sally tends to a desperately wounded child in the back of her ambulance during her second evacuation from East Mostar after the UN refused to allow the evacuees into their base.

PART TWO

Life on the Line

8

THE GATES ARE BARRED

I thought all my troubles were over as, mission accomplished, I drove away from Mostar with my precious cargo and back towards Medugorje but the UN had one last rebuff up its sleeve. As I pulled up at the base I saw what seemed like hundreds of photographers and TV cameramen waiting at the gates with soldiers holding them back. I drove through into the compound and we began carrying the children inside as the press clambered on the gates to get a better view.

A Spanish officer asked me to leave so that the press would go too. I asked if I might say goodbye to the children first but he refused. As I walked slowly and sadly away, Sky's Christopher Morris who had overheard the exchange, tackled the officer in his own language. I was called back and told I could see the children after all.

Overjoyed I rushed into the small clinic where each had been allocated a bed and where they were all eating happily. I kissed each child gently but brushed away their thanks which only embarrassed me. After all these children had a right to be treated with humanity and simple dignity. It was not something they should have to be grateful for.

Outside in between live interviews on satellite for Sky and CNN I was able to hug Lynne and Ivan who had waited anxiously for my return. I took Ivan's hand in mine and looked deep into his eyes. '*You* made this possible,' I said. 'Thank you.'

A few days later, when I hoped the East Mostar doctors would have had time to stabilise the three wounded children I had promised to go back for, I prepared to set off again. The image of their blood-covered bodies had haunted me ever since I saw them in the car park and I was anxious to keep my word.

I had been to the UN base to make sure they were aware of this evacuation and would be ready to receive the children. I also asked them to send a message to the Muslim authorities to warn them of my journey. Lynne meanwhile had gone to every organisation in the area asking for someone to take care of the children once they arrived.

I was also able to speak to my mother and father via a breakfast television link. My mother was thrilled and even my father, not normally a man given to public displays of emotion, said how proud and pleased he was with what I had done. The Sky crew had a whip round and gave me fifty pounds to buy supplies for the doctors.

Lynne however was not so lucky. None of the agencies, including the Red Cross, would agree to take responsibility for the children. I was not overly concerned. I knew the UN could always arrange the onward journey to Split or Zagreb as they had done with the first evacuees who were now at the American Mobile Army Surgical Hospital in Zagreb.

Ivan arrived with new documents and the old ambulance. He also brought along a signed document enabling Tim, a Suncokret volunteer who would be my guide and translator, to join me. Tim was sociable and enthusiastic and I was glad of his company. He also knew the way, having been in East Mostar a few months before.

A couple of TV crews filmed our departure and as we pulled away it occurred to me that millions of people now knew about this trip which made me feel much safer than I had the first time.

Again we had a police escort as far as the front line. The old airport was still bathed in light and all seemed quiet as we reached the railway barrier checkpoint. This time it was unmanned and Tim stepped down to open it. A few metres further on a small group of soldiers appeared and stepped in front of the ambulance, their guns pointed towards us. At first I was not too bothered, thinking it was simply a new checkpoint but then they directed us into the yard of an abandoned building and ordered us out.

Tim tried to explain who we were but for all his pleasant manner he spoke the language little better than Paul and the soldiers shook their heads in incomprehension. Finally I managed to understand from one who spoke a little German that they wanted us to see their commander. Yet again it seemed there had been some mix-up in informing the Muslim authorities. I refused to leave the ambulance, afraid we would never see it again, and to their obvious annoyance I clung stubbornly to the keys until they agreed to let me drive it to their command post.

The soldiers walked in front leading us off the main road and down a slope that led to the old railway track. Half way down I stopped, fearing that we would get stuck in the rough terrain but their leader insisted we press on. Within minutes my fears were realised: the vehicle became embedded in the loose stones and no amount of accelerating or reversing would shift it.

Suddenly to our horror we heard the sound of machine-gun fire. It seemed to be all around us. The soldiers took cover behind an abandoned train carriage and signalled for us to do the same. We crouched by its enormous old wheels for what seemed like an eternity.

'Why are they doing this?' I cried to Tim who shook his head, no wiser than I was as to which side was aiming at us.

One of the soldiers disappeared down the slope and came back with an older man who we could tell from his dress and demeanour was obviously a commander of some sort. He could speak no English either and we were again driven to sign language. I showed him my HVO document and some sort of light seemed to dawn on his face for he signalled towards the ambulance and rocked his arms as if he were cradling a baby. Yes, yes, I nodded; at last someone who understood.

Ducking low to avoid the bullets he raced to the ambulance and struggled desperately to move it. His head was in full sight and I fully expected him to be killed at any moment. He was unused to the gears and try as he may he could not get it into reverse. I had no choice but to leave my cover and join him.

I felt sick with fear. A bullet could come through the windscreen any second. I shoved the gear stick into reverse, again to no avail. The commander called for one of his men who raced bent double to a nearby outbuilding while I ran back to the cover of the carriage. Tim was white with shock and stared at me helplessly as I raged against our unknown and unseen attackers.

The soldiers returned with a spade and courageously – they were directly in the line of fire – began to dig out the wheels. At last the ambulance was free and Tim and I dashed over to it. The commander offered to drive. I accepted gratefully: I did not think my nerves could stand any more. I told Tim to get in the back where there were no windows and I sat alongside the commander as he inched the vehicle up the slope.

We hit the open road and he put his foot to the floor. As he drove I leaned as far back in my seat as possible until I realised that if a bullet missed me it would surely hit him so I forced myself forward again to give this brave man some protection. He was an excellent driver, fast and skilful, and when we reached the city he insisted on taking us right up to the hospital. All I could give him were a couple of cartons of cigarettes and my gratitude. He said he would wait and drive us out as well.

Inside the hospital where the doctors looked surprised and delighted to see us I sent a message to the last Jewish family remaining in East Mostar. They arrived within twenty minutes: an elderly couple called August and Erna Cipra. I also met another woman who was Jewish herself but married to a Muslim. She and her two small children would not leave without him and he needed special papers. Once again I found myself saying I would come back, this time with appropriate documentation for him.

August and Erna had packed just one small bag. Nearly everything they owned, including their home, was being left behind but they were eager to leave the city and join their children in Croatia.

I was saddened to learn that one of the children I had come for, the elder boy, had died within two hours of the last evacuation. For all their skills the doctors had been unable to save him with the limited equipment they had available. But there was another boy: an eleven-year-old who was now lying in a coma. By a near miracle the neurosurgeon had managed to

91

save his life after a bullet pierced his brain but he would die without the more extensive treatment only available in the outside world. The problem was he could not be moved immediately, he needed a little more time before his evacuation could be risked.

His family kept a round-the-clock vigil at his bedside, holding his hand and talking to him though they could not know whether he was even aware of their presence. They begged me to take him. I looked into their desperate faces and gave them the little reassurance I could: I would try. The neurosurgeon took my hand in his.

'They call you the Angel of Mostar,' he said, 'and you are. You are our hope for the future. I am honoured to know you.'

I was touched by his words and proud. Many times in my past I had wondered about my purpose in life and now I had the answer. I knew that, even if I never did anything else, this had made my life worthwhile.

We left the city just as darkness fell: the mother and her two surviving children plus her elderly mother and August and Erna. Tim was in the back attending to them. The commander who had insisted on having his photograph taken with me before we set off was driving. Thankfully the journey was peaceful and we dropped him off where we had first met him.

After crossing the runway I took what I thought was the correct turn I needed to meet up with our police escort but it was dark and everything looked different. Suddenly a large group of HVO soldiers forced us to a halt. They were scruffy and dirty with faces taut from stress and lack of sleep. They had obviously been at the front line for a long time and I was worried about their reactions to a group of Muslims.

They forced back the door and peered inside. The young

mother clutched her baby and stared blankly into their fierce faces. She was too traumatised to know or care what was happening. Her mother was beside her stroking the child's hand. August and Erna looked extremely calm given the circumstances. Just as the soldiers began insisting that we all get out I spotted a familiar face. It was one of our policemen. I did not know when I was ever so glad to see someone. He dismissed the angry looking group of armed men and we followed him back to safety.

Lynne and a couple of newspaper reporters were waiting for us outside the UN base. I asked the soldier on guard to open the gates. He refused. I was astonished. The gates were barred to wounded children and frightened, tired civilians. I looked around. There was no sign of life, none of the expected aid or refuge organisations; just a long dark empty road.

Several Spanish officers came out and made it clear they would have nothing to do with my patients. I pleaded with them to provide food and drink at least and eventually someone brought out water and yoghurt. Then to my immense relief Sky television arrived on the scene.

The reporter trained her camera on one of the officers and spoke slowly and clearly. 'This is an ambulance,' she said. 'An ambulance with sick children inside.'

'I don't understand,' he muttered and turned his back.

Frustration had been welling up inside me and now I vented it on television. As the camera turned to me I launched an attack on the UN and all the other organisations whose policies were so rigid they could not encompass emergency assistance to wounded children. I had risked my own life crossing a front line to rescue them and now no one would take over at this end.

93

These were organisations funded by the tax-payer or by charitable donations, I continued in anger. The public wanted its money spent on people in need not on maintaining unwieldy bureaucracies.

My outburst was reported world-wide to the huge embarrassment of the United Nations and the aid organisations. To be caught literally ignoring the cries of children in need was not good public relations. Inevitably they denied all knowledge of my mission saying I had not informed them and they were unprepared. But that was untrue: both Lynne and I knew how hard we had pushed.

Finally an urgent message from Lynne brought Ivan and a group of colleagues to the base. They had a fully equipped ambulance into which the patients were carefully transferred and then driven to Split. All this was caught on camera too: Croatian doctors saving enemy lives while the UN stood by and did nothing.

I was pestered all night by calls from the media and in the end I had to put a stop to it. I was desperate for sleep and I had new promises to keep.

Firstly though I decided to return to Britain for a few days proper rest and to arrange more supplies. On my way through Split I called in at the hospital to check on 'my patients'. The boy was doing fine, he had had his operation and his sight had been saved. I was thrilled. As I bent down to speak to him he said something I could not understand and I asked one of the doctors to translate.

The doctor shifted uneasily. 'He says he wants you to get out of the way because you're blocking his view of his mother.'

The staff gave me a posy and a book on Croatia and the people on the streets pointed and waved. It was extraordinary.

I had become a celebrity for saving the lives of their enemy.

Back in Britain though I faced a very different welcome. There was such a throng of pressmen at Heathrow I had to be steered through by police but it was not until later that I understood the full picture. Apparently one of the Spanish officers who had been trapped with the convoy in East Mostar had alleged that I was a spy and had offered the UN secret information in return for an armoured car, ammunition, boots and a compass.

My first reaction was to laugh but when I saw how much attention his claims had been getting – the *Daily Mirror* even ran a front page story under the headline UN SIGNS SALLY'S DEATH WARRANT – I became seriously worried. This could endanger me personally and threaten any future operations. Each side would now be wondering whether I really was betraying them. I knew no secrets because I had never been interested in political moves or military strategy, only in the victims of war, but the situation in Bosnia was too tense for me to allow such allegations to go unchallenged.

Chris Morris spoke up for me on Sky and commended my actions and then I had my own chance to put the record straight on the live phone-in programme *Talkback*. The questions were interesting and challenging. Almost every caller congratulated me and I knew then that whatever the slurs, the majority of the public were behind me.

One woman complained that I had not helped Serb children but I told her I had not asked to see passports. It did not matter to me which side they came from and I would have helped all of them if it had been possible. Another caller, speaking from Rome, suggested that we should leave the Balkans to their fate and remained unmoved by my arguments that innocent people would die if aid agencies pulled out. I ended the discussion with my answer to the claim that I had done everything purely for publicity. If that was all I was after I said I would have climbed the Post Office Tower naked.

During my week in Britain I was given a cheque for five hundred pounds by the International Committee of Jewish Women for the community in Mostar to spend on their New Year. I also received payment for an exclusive in the *Daily Mirror* about my clashes with the UN. From this I was able to pay back Peter Kates and buy various things for particular individuals as well as general items. I bought Erna some of her beloved art materials as well as clothes for Damir, Stipe and Zoran. I also packed plenty of vitamins, baby medicines and warm shawls for the old women. It was not very long to the time when their problems would be magnified a thousand-fold by the bitter cold of the Balkan winter.

9

SHOCKS AND SHELLS

A crew from the American network ABC met me on my return to Split. They were making a documentary called *Heroes* about ordinary people who risked their lives to help others and they were interested in the fact that I was to try and evacuate Selma's father, Mirzad Handzjar. The little girl had been flown on to the States from Zagreb with her mother and little brother and everyone wanted to see the family reunited.

The cameraman was a sturdy South African called Roger. He was accompanied by a young Bosnian, half Croat, half Muslim, with the unlikely name of Elvis who was to be the translator and 'fixer'. When they said they would be following me into East Mostar in an armoured vehicle I half hoped my patients would be able to ride in it on the return journey but unfortunately the crew were forbidden to assist the actual operation in any way.

When we reached the Čitluk Hotel Lynne was in a terrible state. She had spent the week avoiding the horrible Eddo. Before I left I had asked Ivan to keep an eye on him but unfortunately he had taken my request to the extreme. He had had Eddo arrested for drunkenness, relieved of his weapons and suspended from duty with the result that he spent every moment of his time in the hotel. Ivan and the other doctors were often out and Collette and the Boys were away so the terrified Lynne had only felt safe locked in her room.

Tim called from Zagreb and begged to come with me again. ABC were delighted at the chance of a genuine American hero. Unfortunately getting permission for any of us to go was much more difficult this time. The fighting in Mostar had intensified of late as each side pushed harder and harder in a desperate battle for territory and emotions were running high.

Many people were directing their anger at foreigners like myself. *I* knew the Croatian medical authorities had been behind my missions; I knew too that I had seized every opportunity to keep my word to Ivan and publicise the problems of Nova Bila hospital and that there had even been an evacuation from there partly as a result of my efforts. But for those who did not know the facts I was simply someone who had helped the other side.

In such circumstances the obviously Muslim Handzjar – literally old Turkish dagger – was not a good surname to have on a list for transit visas. A soldier who was hanging around the hotel reception desk while we were checking the list spotted it and launched into a tirade of abuse. Whenever he saw us afterwards he would spit out the words 'You help Muslims.'

None of this bothered me too much apart from the worry that it mght affect future plans but Lynne was deeply upset. Until now she had known and liked this young man. She did not know how long she could tolerate the atmosphere and we both reluctantly agreed that it might be better if she went home afer the next mission. In the meantime Collette and Sean would look after her while I was away.

The situation grew ever more confused. Ivan was away in Zagreb and his colleague, Vava, was helping me sort out the visas and other documents. Vava was to become my great friend and protector, a tall, slim man with an open, friendly face and a broad smile. He had short, straight hair which he continually tried to flatten. It defied his best efforts, however, and sprang up in tufts. Although he ran the Siroci Brig radio station, he was in actual fact an artist and writer who spoke several languages fluently, including English with an American accent. Vava generated laughter around him as he took on the role of court jester for Ivan and his medical colleagues. He would do the most incredibly accurate impressions of people, especially of Ivan who he teased mercilessly about looking like Gaddaffi's brother. Ironically, he resembled an Arab with his jet black hair and dark skin. Throughout that week he stayed at the Čitluk, keeping my spirits up when it seemed I would never receive permission for the operation.

We still could not get any guarantee of a ceasefire and I was told I would not be able to make the journey on the day I had hoped. Suddenly I got a phone call: I could go after all, the next day.

The whole thing seemed very dubious – what was all this to-ing and fro-ing about? – but the TV crew were getting impatient and I did not want them to abandon the project. This would be the first evacuation involving a Muslim man and all its attendant dangers and I felt a TV camera might be the only protection we would have. I certainly had no illusions left about the UN. I knew the other side would not be forewarned of our arrival but I hoped they would at least recognise the ambulance from the two previous trips. A decision had to be made and I made it: we would take our chances early next day.

A shy English lad who worked in a bakery in Medugorje and who wanted now to do something worthwhile offered to come with us. I accepted his offer: I felt I needed all the help I could get. He was also named Tim but being the taller of the two I called him Big Tim to distinguish him from the American.

He brought with him the bonus of two borrowed flak jackets and helmets and we agreed the Tims would have these. I had borrowed a white, supposedly bullet-proof vest from a soldier. The men's cost around a thousand pounds as opposed to three hundred for mine but theirs were navy like the UN's. I preferred white in the hope that from a distance I would look like a member of a medical team.

Eddo came down to see us off. He was dressed in full kit and his weapons were back in his possession: he had been taken back into the brigade and was off to join them at the front. For some strange reason he presented me with a stack of personal photos and his wedding ring to look after until he returned – or did not return. I passed them quietly over to Lynne; I did not want the responsibility of them in a war zone. He kissed my cheek, smiled a toothless smile and wished me luck. Considering I was a Jew, he said, he liked me very much and saluted dramatically. I drove away laughing.

The trip was uneventful until we reached the outskirts of East Mostar where we took a wrong turn and ended up high above the area we were aiming for. A burst of artillery fire rang out and I quickly pulled the ambulance behind a block of flats. Gradually people began to creep out on to their balconies to peer down at us. Children called out, probably for the sweets they had seen UN convoys throw out as they passed.

A man standing on the pavement was willing to show us the way and climbed into the ambulance. We drove down a narrow road and I began to relax, relieved to have a guide. The crack of a sniper's rifle shattered my composure and sheared off the blue light on top of the ambulance. There was only one way to go and that was straight on into a tunnel. I screeched into it but the roof was too low and the ambulance stuck fast. Each time I tried to move the roof scraped against the tunnel ceiling with a hideous grinding noise. I could not go forward but reversing meant presenting the sniper with a perfect target.

All our lives depended on my decision. I felt a sense of panic rise in me. With one swift move I thrust the gear stick into reverse and pressed my foot hard to the floor. It sounded as if the roof were being torn off like a sardine tin as I pushed further and further backwards until we were out of the tunnel but into the sights of the gunman. Now I had to somehow turn the vehicle around so we could get away.

I shunted back and forth in the narrow street in what felt like a fifty-point turn as the bullets whistled past. My heart was pumping so hard I thought it would force its way out of my chest but at last I was able to pull away and round a corner out of the sniper's sights. I was still trembling as we reached the city centre. Roger and Elvis were not far behind in their more manoeuvrable jeep. Our guide who must surely have regretted his offer of help took us as far as the hospital. I reached for a couple of cartons of cigarettes and coffee but he grabbed my arm: 'You, woman who saves our children. You good. We know.'

Inside the hospital our reception was less than warm. Almost immediately, Dr Mellovic, the doctor in charge, a very tall, healthy-looking, bearded man came up to me and told me that I was not welcome, that I was a traitor. I assumed at first that he was referring to the UN officer's spying allegations but Hafid, the neurosurgeon, took me to one side and explained.

Croatian television had used my missions, especially the last one, as propaganda. There were pictures of Ivan and the others helping the children into their ambulance and I was quoted as saying that the Croats had helped save the lives of East Mostar children. The mother had been shown thanking the HVO.

The local BIH commander, General Pashalic, had been enraged by the film and insisted the woman had been forced to say those words at gunpoint. Mellovic had been given a dressing down and told no more patients would be evacuated in future without Pashalic's express permission.

I insisted on another meeting with Mellovic and spent a long time trying to persuade him of the truth. Eventually with the help of a woman doctor with near-perfect English I managed to convince him. But he remained adamant that only BIH command could consent to any evacuation.

Elvis agreed to come with me to the Muslim forces' headquarters as did young Tim. Just as we were setting off Selma's father, Mirzad, arrived and insisted on joining us. He had just heard via the Red Cross that his family were safe in America and the happiness was clearly visible on his weather-beaten face. Underneath though he was a desperate man and made it clear that he would leave with me whether he had official permission or not.

The general would not be available for another two hours and not wanting to negotiate the snipers' alleyways any more than necessary we decided to wait. As we sat on the porch of the command building I surveyed the damage caused by two years of shelling, first by Serbian forces, then by Croatian.

Few buildings had escaped entirely and many were reduced to a pile of rubble. Not far away were three UN armoured personnel carriers manned by Spanish soldiers. They had stayed behind at the Bosnians' insistence when the convoy was finally allowed to leave in the hope they might afford some protection.

As the evening drew near Elvis became fidgety. 'I'm not spending the night here,' he said. 'If we haven't sorted this out by eight o'clock we'll have to leave.'

'There's no way I'm going without the people I came for,' I said, 'not after all this. I'll wait until tomorrow if necessary.'

At last a brand new Suzuki jeep drew up and the general got out. A tall, good-looking man in his late forties he strode past us without a word. He was a hero in the area for the way in which he had held off the enemy for so long but he did not seem an heroic figure to me. To me he was a man using wounded children as pawns in a propaganda war. Yet I also understood how, having fought for so long under such desperate conditions, the sight of one of his own people saying thank you to the enemy must have upset morale. After all, it was a shell fired by the HVO that had killed her son and seriously wounded her other two children.

Shortly afterwards Elvis was summoned in. He was only gone five minutes and when he returned it was clear from his face that the news was bad. Not only would Mirzad Handzjar not be allowed to leave without an American visa, the Muslim husband of the Jewish woman would have to have a visa from Israel. As for the children they were not the general's concern: I would have to go to the war office. Oh and something else – he had a personal message for me.

'Tell her she ought to be in prison,' he said to Elvis.

It was just the kind of encouraging remark I needed. We returned dejectedly to the hospital. Elvis was concerned for my safety if I remained in the city but by this stage I was damned if I was going to be thwarted by one man's prejudice and bloodymindedness. Hafid politely offered me his bed for the night but I declined seeing how exhausted he was.

Instead I went upstairs where there were several spare beds awaiting a new team of doctors coming in across the mountains from Sarajevo. The Tims slept in the ambulance, Elvis and Roger in the jeep. All of us had a night troubled by the distant thump of shells and awoke anxious to get the evacuation over as soon as possible.

Meanwhile, in West Mostar, Vava who was waiting anxiously at Bielje Brig hospital for my return, received a phone call from my mother. Trying to calm his fears for my safety he had just drunk six bottles of beer when she rang to ask how I was.

'How's Sally?' she asked. Vava replied as casually as he could, 'she's fine, she should be coming out in the morning.' My mother cheerfully asked him to send me her love. 'I will' said Vava and reached for another bottle.

I was at the war office on the dot of eight. I had one other card up my sleeve, a letter of introduction from Stipe Rozic to an old school friend who worked there. I was to check his bona fides by asking him which beach he and Stipe had gone to as teenagers. If he answered correctly I would know he was the right man and could be trusted with a letter from someone now regarded as the enemy.

I asked for the man by name and asked my question. He gave me the right answer and I handed over the letter. The response, however, seemed all too familiar.

'Firstly,' he said, 'it is impossible to do anything for Mr Handzjar. He is of fighting age and although wounded in the leg cannot be released. The husband of the Jewish lady is also still liable for military service and the only way he can go is with proof from Israel that he will be going there. His wife and children are of course free to travel.'

'But she will not go without him,' I protested.

'Then she is a fool,' he said.

'Well, what about the children in the hospital?' I cried. 'What about Marijana? She was wounded recently and she's only eleven and the doctors say she could die if she doesn't get proper treatment soon.'

The words kept pouring out. 'What about the boy who's in a coma? And the woman with a head wound? And her son? He's going to lose his arm if he's not operated on quickly.'

The man lowered his voice as if he did not want to be heard by anyone outside.

'Maybe if you wait two, three days. Then we make sure the children have the right documentation and could leave safely.'

But they would be safe anyway, I told him, struggling to control my voice. The Croats had proved they were not out to harm my evacuees.

'Either you wait and help the children,' he said flatly, 'or you leave.'

There was no point in arguing further: at least he had not refused outright. As he showed me out I asked if there was anywhere I could buy cigarettes. I had not expected to be staying so long and had given all mine away. He took me to a small room and opened the door. The walls were stacked high with cartons of them. There had been an attempt to hide the brand name but it could still be read on the sides. They were called Yugoslavia. The cigarettes were obviously as old as their name for they tasted foul. But they would do. This was no situation in which to try giving up smoking.

Back at the hospital I told the others the news. Elvis was adamant that he would not be staying; Roger wanted to give it a little longer and I left them to argue it out. Both Tims had decided to pull out and I did not try to dissuade them: it would be wrong to ask them to risk their lives further. They would go when the UN changed shift next day.

I went in wearily and lay down on Hafid's bed, one of four in a section of the dining room partitioned by a flimsy curtain. The doctors from Sarajevo had arrived and all the beds upstairs were full. Hafid insisted his bed was mine for as long as I stayed. He had been much cheered by the news I had brought him that his wife was in good health and being well looked after.

My head sank back on to the pillow and I closed my eyes. For a few seconds there was an ominous whine and then an enormous blast shook the building as a rocket-propelled grenade exploded in front of the window just feet away from my bed. The few pieces of glass left from previous attacks hurtled into the room and dust billowed over everything. All I could think of was whether the ceiling would cave in.

Slowly I opened my eyes. The bed and the blanket which was over my body were covered in a layer of broken glass. Slowly I began pulling slivers of glass from my skin and I could feel tiny rivulets of blood trickling down my face and mingling with the white dust.

I ran out into the corridor. Dr Mellovic's three-year-old son was sitting on the bloodstained floor and I crouched down beside him. Another shell hit the building and I jumped at the noise. The boy giggled delightedly. He had never before seen anyone jump at the bangs which to him were part of everyday life. Each time the building was hit I reacted with the same involuntary start and each time he laughed with glee.

A young woman was carried into the corridor from the street outside and laid at the far end among the other casualties who had arrived the previous night. I could hear her cries echoing through the space between us. After a while the moans stopped and I asked someone if she had been given painkillers.

'We don't have any painkillers,' came the reply, 'and anyway she doesn't need them now. She's dead.'

10

TRAPPED

I felt as if I had entered hell. Sixty-five shells hit the hospital in the first twenty-four hours and the stream of casualties seemed endless: men and women, boys and girls, babies. Their screams and cries filled the air. Many died even as they waited for treatment.

Hafid ran from operation to operation like a man possessed, his green uniform covered in blood, his eyes frantic. Mellovic was the first to see each patient and he would look at me and murmur 'Your friends did this.' I had no answer.

Roger had rushed off with some soldiers to film the action but returned unscathed. Elvis who was waiting anxiously for him at the entrance was hit in the back by a burst of shrapnel. I watched as a doctor extracted the jagged shards and thought how poor Elvis somehow summed up the whole mess that was Bosnia. Here were his father's people firing upon his mother's people and injuring him.

They left the next morning with the UN during a lull in the onslaught and I gave them a note for Lynne. I felt at that moment that I might not survive this mission and I was glad I had left a letter with a friend back in England to be given to my parents if I did not return. It would tell them all the things I wanted them to know.

I passed the hours visiting patients and talking to the staff. I was feeling far from well myself. I suffer from a condition known as hiatus hernia for which you are advised to eat little and often but that had been difficult before and was impossible now. The food at the hospital consisted of dry bread for breakfast, a plate of stodgy rice and gravy for lunch and the same for dinner, washed down with homemade 'coffee' made from green beans. It tasted nothing like coffee but at least it was brown and hot and a thousand times better than the dirty water from the river which was stored in a plastic container in the kitchen.

Either the food or the water disagreed with me and my stomach became distended and extremely painful, a condition made worse by the fact that I could only bring myself to use the filthy toilet – it was the only facility for fifty patients and all the staff and there was no water to flush it – when absolutely necessary.

Hafid found me curled up in pain and suggested an operation. His offer, though well intended, seemed absurd under the circumstances and I declined. I knew how busy he was with the casualties and besides I did not fancy my chances in such conditions. Instead I stopped eating altogether which seemed to ease the pain a little. I lost weight dramatically. From a borderline size between twelve and fourteen I shrank rapidly to barely a size ten.

A man came to see me on behalf of the two hundred Albanians in Mostar, wanting me to pass on a message to their embassy. He came several times to remind me, risking his life every time. On hearing of his arrival for the fifth time I burst out in exasperation: 'I've said I'll do what I can.'

'You don't understand,' said the cook who had delivered the message. 'He was killed by a sniper. It's his body they've brought in.'

Mellovic asked me whether I would like to speak on Radio Mostar. I declined. The last thing I wanted was to be drawn further into the propaganda war. But I did agree they could mention my presence at the hospital: he seemed to think it might stop the Croats shelling the building. I was sure it would make no difference but I guessed it could do no harm.

That day he took me to the bedside of a young Croat who had been hit in the stomach while working as a prisoner on the front line. He needed several pints of blood or he would die but the hospital had none of his particular group. He was only twenty-one and seemed already near to death. I put my hand on his burning forehead and he reached weakly for it, staring up at me from feverish eyes.

All I could suggest was that Mellovic write directly to Ivan Bagaric. There were four other HVO soldiers who had been caught in the same blast. Perhaps they might stop firing on the hospital if they knew their own men were inside.

The Tims, pale and drawn and covered in dust, were on the point of leaving so I gave them his letter to pass on to Ivan. When they had gone I felt suddenly very alone. Hafid seemed my only friend now, the only one who spoke English and made time for a conversation.

The day after the Tims left I went to visit the young soldier again. He took my hand and squeezed it with what remained of his strength, murmuring, 'let's go, let's go,' over and over again as my eyes filled with tears. The next day a small UNPROFOR contingent arrived with a doctor to evacuate him.

Even though their appearance was probably due to his letter

to Ivan, Mellovic flew into a rage. He had, he shouted, given them a list of seriously wounded children fifteen days before but they would not come for them, no they would only come for a fighting man, and he ordered them out of the building.

The news of my presence was broadcast and by coincidence the shelling of the hospital stopped. That relieved the situation in one way but it also meant the war office were in no rush to see me leave.

Death had become a part of everyday life. No one who left the building could be sure of returning alive. I worried especially about Hafid who set off every night to feed a cat which had belonged to his father and still lived in the ruins of the house. He kept half his food ration for his sister and niece who lived in the basement of the local pharmacy. All I could do was give him the food I was not eating and a powerful torch.

During daylight I would run from the hospital to the war office seeking the precious departure papers but it was either closed or I would be told to come back tomorrow. It was the most frustrating time I had ever known, made even more so by the fact that every day the poor families or the children themselves would ask me when we were leaving.

The shelling continued round the clock and we watched the carnage on the nightly news. There were loud cheers when the newscaster announced that the Muslim counter-offensive had gained ground but then on to the screen came pictures of a massacre of Bosnian Croats by Muslim soldiers, including the horrific sight of a young boy stabbed to death.

'They are all as bad as each other in the end,' said Hafid softly.

On the fifth day I was woken by a French accent and pulling back the curtain I saw Danielle from UNICEF. We rushed to embrace each other. Unfortunately she was just leaving, she had come in with a small convoy led by the head of the United Nations High Commission for Refugees in Bosnia called Jerry Hulme, and they were setting off any minute. When I explained my position she insisted I meet him. I raced after her through the alleyways to where the convoy was parked and quickly I blurted out my story. After hearing it Jerry Hulme agreed to return with the necessary transport.

As I watched them pull out I felt more alone than ever. I longed to go with them away from all this death and destruction, back to the safety of Čitluk. But my conscience would not let me. I had come this far, I had to see it through. I walked back to the hospital, running only where necessary. I was light-headed with the lack of food and mildly feverish and the sun beating down on my head made me feel even worse.

That night a shell hit my ambulance knocking out the engine. No one dared fix it so I was now without transport. It was the final straw. Now, even if I did receive permission, I had no way of evacuating the children. There was no option but to return alone.

I went to lie down on Hafid's bed and he joined me, lying stiffly alongside in case I should misinterpret his motives. He said that he felt wretched about my treatment but he was powerless. I told him not to worry, that Jerry Hulme would return for the children, and the next morning I tried explaining that to the patients.

I went to see the little boy who would lose his arm without treatment, sitting patiently beside his mother who had a serious head wound. I saw the father of a sixteen-year old girl who had suffered a spinal injury and the parents of Hafid's patient who were still keeping vigil at his bedside. I climbed the stairs to another ward where Marijana, the eleven-year-old girl was lying on the floor as there were no more beds. She grinned at me as I approached, seeming unaware of her stomach wound where she'd been hit by shrapnel. The doctor had assured me she would recover but I was concerned by the dreadfully insanitary conditions in which she was lying. As I turned to leave the room where the wounded lay side by side I assured those within earshot that I'd be back. 'I promise' I said, before walking away.

I gave the Tims' flak jackets to the stretcher bearers who continually risked death in their dash for the wounded. They were not mine to give away but I could think of no more deserving recipients. Hafid was operating so I was unable to say goodbye to him but I left a note on his bed with thanks for all his generosity and kindness and a promise that I would see his wife got the baby things she needed. I handed the keys of my ambulance to Mellovic's wife and ran from the hospital in tears.

Over at the armoured personnel carriers I waited for the Spanish officer to fax base for permission to bring me out with the change of guard. As I sat on the pavement a scrawny puppy padded warily towards me. He was a dirty white with dark patches and an enormous head and he held an injured paw in the air. I reached over to him and tried to see if he had trodden on something. Sensing that I meant no harm he licked my face.

Suddenly I was overwhelmed. Burying my face against his neck, still silky despite the dirt, I broke down in bitter tears. I wept for this poor hungry animal so unused to kindness and for all the wretched creatures of this once beautiful city, for all the people and their children, who lived day after day in dank basements, thin and pale and sad.

I rode away from the city inside an armoured personnel

carrier. It was small and cramped but it felt wonderfully safe. That comfort was not to last. We broke down before we even cleared the outskirts and had to be pushed from behind by another. A journey that should have taken forty minutes lasted seven hours. The soldiers asked me to go on to Medugorje rather than stop at Čitluk.

By the time I finally got out I was weak and shaking. The fresh air hit me in a rush and I fainted. I came to surrounded by people and cameras. A microphone was pushed under my nose as I staggered towards the clinic. 'How does it feel,' came the question, 'to be rescued by the UN?'

Back at the hotel I was greeted by Lynne and Ivan who had been sick with worry. Ivan had been to church every day to pray for my safety and had barely slept. For two hours he and his colleagues questioned me about my week in enemy territory although to be fair they were not seeking military information, merely some explanation of how the trip had gone so horribly wrong.

I was tired out, my head throbbed badly and I looked awful. My cheeks were hollow, there were dark shadows beneath my eyes and my clothes were filthy and bloodstained. Collette pushed her way through the men and insisted I get some sleep. She ushered me into her own room. She thought I was slightly concussed and should be kept under observation. She made me some camomile tea and I slipped beneath the clean fresh sheets. No bullets, no shelling, no screams of pain. Only Collette's cool hand on my forehead when she checked me every four hours and the soft sound of Sean's breathing across the room.

AGE SHALL NOT WEARY THEM

As soon as I was well enough I went to see Ivan about blood supplies for the wounded soldier back in East Mostar and suggested he give them to Jerry Hulme. I had donated my own while I was there but it was the wrong type for the soldier. I also saw Jerry himself who assured me the promised evacuation would take place within days. In the meantime he would be going in with a Medivac team to assess the patients. This seemed to me an unnecessary extra stage but Jerry seemed a genuine sort of man, if a little patronising in his manner and anyway I had no say in the matter.

Then he asked me for a favour. Would I use my influence with Ivan to get permission for himself and Danielle to look at the Croat hospitals and orphanages in West Mostar? Ivan agreed on the condition that I accompany them. It seemed ironic considering my increasingly fraught relationship with the UN that I was now to be cast in the role of chaperone.

A rather odd character had recently arrived on the scene. Known as Big Rod because of his size he had driven from Britain in his own customised armoured ambulance with the express purpose of helping my evacuation. Unfortunately he was a man with a short temper and he did not like what he heard about the delays. Jerry Hulme, who had come to collect me for the trip to the orphanages, caught the full force of his wrath.

Unless those children were out within a few days, he roared, waving his fist, he would see to it personally that the media knew all about UN incompetence. Jerry looked terribly embarrassed by the scene and muttered some comment about the strange company I kept as we got into his landrover. At least, I thought to myself, compared to the likes of Big Rod I must seem mild-mannered.

While Jerry and Danielle toured West Mostar hospital I went down to visit Damir and his family. Poor Damir had been trying to get to Britain where he had relatives but had only got as far as Zagreb: apparently he could not leave without his parents. Erna and Stipe had no wish to become refugees themselves so the poor boy had no choice but to return to his home on the front line.

They seemed in good spirits however. Erna had begun teaching herself English. Her father was out of hospital thanks to the antibiotics I had brought and was even starting to walk again. She told me how she had heard people in the street discussing the Angel of Mostar. 'I told them you are our friend. So now I am very popular. Because I know the famous Sally Becker.'

We all laughed but Damir assured me it was true and indeed when I passed the checkpoint beneath their apartment I noticed how the soldiers vied with each other to light my cigarette and direct me through.

It was even happening in Čitluk. We were constantly having to turn down invitations to people's homes. The hotel receptionists who had hitherto treated us with indifference were now very respectful. I think it was partly because I had been over to the 'other side' and lived to tell the tale and partly because I had helped draw the world's attention to Mostar. It was some comfort to people to know they were not forgotten.

Three days after my return, Collette, Sean and a couple of the Boys went down to West Mostar. Before she set off Collette made me promise to take her back with me to East Mostar when I next returned: she wanted to offer her skills to the hospital there. Sean had been against the idea at first but when he saw how much it meant to her he decided he would go too.

It was never to be. Collette was hit that day by a burst of shrapnel in West Mostar. A rocket-propelled grenade blasted through the room in which she was standing. Sean who had been in the doorway was hurled backwards by the explosion. As he picked himself up he saw Collette clutching her stomach trying to hold together the appalling wound. The shrapnel had ripped open her abdomen and torn her vital organs. Knowing how seriously injured she was, she was fighting to control her breathing, trying desperately to stop herself bleeding to death.

Sean held her all the way to the hospital and paced the corridor outside the operating theatre while doctors battled for four hours to save Collette's life in the building where she had helped to save others. Now he had been sent home to wait and to tell the story none of us wanted to hear.

Someone led him downstairs for a drink and Tim suggested I read the Tarot. I laid out the pack more as a distraction from the dreadful waiting than anything else but I still cried out with joy when the cards read favourably. I told Sean when he came back upstairs but he only shrugged and said 'I hope you're right.'

Thierry shook his head and said 'She won't make it. The

wounds are too bad and even if she did, she would be on tubes and machines for the rest of her life. Collette would not want that. She is too alive, too vital to be able to live that way.'

Nobody spoke. We were all shocked by his bluntness. Sean sat silently, staring into space. Just before midnight he said he would go back to his room to put together a few things for the morning. He had only been gone a few minutes when he returned. He put his head round the door and looked straight at me.

'The Tarot lied,' he said. 'She's dead.'

I could not accept what he was saying. It was unthinkable that Collette, beautiful, lively, amusing Collette, was dead. She was only twenty-seven and there was so much she wanted to do.

I could hardly begin to imagine Sean's pain. In the few months they had known each other they had rarely been apart. I remembered how he had gazed at her photograph on that second convoy and how I had teased him. I thought of the poetry he had written, to her and about her, and all the hundreds of photographs he had taken: Collette in her medical greens, in his uniform, by the lake, with the Boys. Collette smiling and laughing. This was all he would have of her now.

He had not eaten all day and we persuaded him to have a tin of creamed rice. He had always loved it and at that moment it was the only comfort we could think of. Then he insisted on returning to the hospital.

I walked out on to the landing, unable to stay in the room alone with my thoughts. I kept thinking how it should have been me. I was the one who had tempted fate over and over again. As I turned to go back into my room I saw one of Ivan's colleagues coming up the stairs. This was a tough man with a normally confident, even jaunty, manner. Tonight he was none of these things. He looked years older and moved slowly and unsurely as if bewildered by grief.

'She was so pretty,' he said and tears ran down his face unchecked. I had been too numb to cry until that moment but now I wept openly too. One of the Boys joined us and we talked long into the night about Collette, remembering funny incidents and amusing things she had said.

Sean had returned to sleep the night in the bed he and Collette had shared and the next morning Thierry took him back to the hospital. Later Thierry told us what had happened.

'It was terrible,' he said. 'They had laid her in a tiny room because the morgue was full. I begged him not to look at her, to leave her covered and to remember her as she was. I have seen so many people die and in this heat and with all the flies I knew it would be bad. But he would not listen. That is not Collette, I told him. That is just a shell. Collette was beautiful.'

We offered to ring her family: it had not been possible to get through before. But Sean insisted he would do it. As I went to leave his room he suddenly reached out his arms. I held him until the tears subsided. There was nothing I could say.

The hospital promised to have a gold plaque made in Collette's honour and mounted on a wall. The health authorities paid for her ashes to be flown back to the States and for Tim and Thierry to accompany Sean. All her friends contributed towards a wreath and with that went the HVO flag so that she should have a guard of honour at her memorial service. As I kissed Sean farewell I could see a spark of light in his eyes again. He had a new mission: to take his beloved home.

A week went by and there was still no date for the evacuation. Rod insisted it would only happen if I did it myself but Ivan was equally adamant that he could not get permission for me to cross the line again. What had happened last time had made them unwilling to take further risks. There was another factor. I had still not managed to keep my word and arrange a similar evacuation for Nova Bila hospital. Ivan's reputation was on the line. Why, his superiors wanted to know, had he let me rescue fifteen Bosnian Muslims when I had done nothing for Bosnian Croats?

I felt I had some stock of credibility left with the Croats because of all the aid and attention I had brought to West Mostar but I realised that could vanish very swiftly if I tried to save any more Muslims without offering similar help to the Croats first.

Things seemed to go from bad to worse. I was told by Jerry Hulme that it might be another two weeks before the evacuation could go ahead. The International Office of Migration (IOM) had taken over the operation which meant beds had to be found in other countries *before* the children could be brought out. It made no sense. I knew Danielle had been able to arrange beds at the MASH hospital as before.

'You've got beds in Zagreb,' I said. 'Why can't the children be taken there and places found for them abroad once they're out of the war zone?'

His answer summed up everything I had come to hate about bureaucracies. 'The IOM don't work like that,' he said. At least he had the good grace to sound embarrassed. 'They prefer to arrange places and visas first.'

'And if people die in the meantime?' I asked angrily.

'That is the way the mandate works,' he said, 'It's their policy.

'Then it's a load of crap,' I cried, 'children are dying because of policies like these. Don't use IOM. Let the UN evacuate the children tomorrow when your convoy goes in.'

He shook his head. 'We had to promise IOM they could take over.'

'Why?' I demanded. This was all a nonsense, a nightmare.

'It's completely out of my hands, it's politics,' he said quietly.

Politics! It was all politics. Politics and publicity. I understood now what was going on. The IOM wanted the kudos of the operation for themselves and they were going to get it even if it meant life-threatening delays. And I knew then that behind all those caring aid workers like Danielle, behind all those brave UN soldiers on the ground, were the faceless puppeteers who pulled the strings for their own political ends. I was consumed with frustration.

I went back to the hotel and broke the news to Rod that the evacuation was definitely off.

'Then I'll do it myself,' he shouted. 'If you've lost your bottle I'll do it myself.'

'And I'll come with you,' Tim piped up from his seat in the lobby.

It was the final straw. I had battled with the Croatian authorities, I had battled with the Muslim authorities, I had battled with the UN. I had had to beg, borrow and scrounge enough money to keep going while highly paid professionals turned their backs. I had been shot at, I had been sick, I had been branded a spy and I had just been forced to spend the most terrifying week of my life in the hell of East Mostar hospital.

And here were two men implying I was somehow giving up. I rounded on them both.

'I'm not going in because I'm not prepared to risk the lives of those children by bringing them through a front line without a ceasefire and I cannot arrange a ceasefire this time because the Croats have had enough of these one-sided operations. If you want to go in, Tim, make sure this time you know the bloody way first.'

Then I shouted at Rod, 'You want to do the big hero bit. Well, make sure it's not at the expense of the children. Not unless you're prepared to live with a child's death on your conscience if it goes wrong.'

Rod was immediately abashed. He was sorry but he was so frustrated at not being able to do anything. I understood his frustration too well. We had been waiting around too long. We all needed to *do* something.

'Look,' I said. 'Tomorrow we'll fill the ambulance with supplies and take them to the warehouse in West Mostar where sixty-seven Jewish people have been waiting patiently for me to fulfil a promise I made several weeks ago. And if you really want to help, take Damir to England.'

We did as we had planned and took great pleasure in spending the money from the ICJW and watching Stipe and Damir unload the supplies into the warehouse. Rod would take Damir to Zagreb and wait with him until a visa was issued. If it was not, he would hide him in his vehicle as far as British immigration where he could seek political asylum. From there he could join his aunt and uncle in Golders Green. I handed the keys of the Renault Four to Erna and Stipe. 'It's yours,' I said.

The Croats had recently set up an embassy in Medugorje and I was invited to lunch with the ambassador. I was then taken to meet Mate Boban, the President of Herzegovina, who congratulated me on what I had achieved in

Mostar – and berated me for what I had failed to do in Central Bosnia.

This was the opportunity I had been looking for. Would he give me permission to take a convoy into East Mostar, I asked, provided I did the same for Nova Bila?

'I don't care where else you go. You can take aid to all sides, give the supplies to whom you want, so long as you include the area of Vitez, Novi Travnic, Bugojno or Nova Bila.'

At last. Now I could realise my dream. I had the President's word on it. But I was looking at something on a much bigger scale than anything I had tackled so far. I would need supplies, transport, volunteers and an enormous amount of money. And I did not have much time: the situation was growing more desperate by the day. I would have to go back to Britain immediately.

As Ivan drove us to the airport I asked him what he thought of Boban.

'He doesn't like me,' Vava translated, 'I was in his office once, discussing the political situation. "Where would you like to be?" he asked me, and I pointed to his chair.'

We all laughed but I wished from the bottom of my heart that Ivan, who really did care about people, had been in that presidential chair. Perhaps then this ugly war would have been over.

As we said goodbye at the airport I gave him a gold ring in the design of the Croatian flag which I had bought in Medugorje. With a smile of delight he slipped it on to the little finger of his bear-like hand. It fitted perfectly.

'It isn't over,' I said to Lynne as we walked towards our plane. 'I'll be back.'

I found a letter from Hafid when I got home. He wrote that I had brought light into his terrible existence and he prayed for my swift return. He thanked me for everything I had done for his people and hoped God would bless me as long as I lived.

He had some terrible news as well. 'I am so sorry to have to tell you that despite their promise to you, the UN did not make the evacuation of our children and the little girl Marijana died of septicaemia. She was only eleven years old. This war is destroying us and killing our children.'

I was overwhelmed by sadness and a sense of guilt and I began to aaccuse myself: I should have been more insistent, I should have gone in regardless, I should have taken the risk.

I dashed off a strongly worded fax to the UN in Zagreb, telling them unless they carried out the evacuation at once I would inform the press of the little girl's death and their part in it. A reply came back the same day: the evacuation would go ahead immediately.

One evening I saw Marijana's mother on a BBC documentary about Mostar. 'Sally Becker said she would rescue my daughter,' she was telling the interviewer, 'but she never came back and my little girl died.'

Her words will haunt me forever.

PART THREE

Operation Angel

12

ONE WOMAN'S DREAM

I scribbled the sums on a piece of paper. We would need, I calculated, about £60,000 to get the convoy to Bosnia and I had arrived back in Britain with about two hundred pounds to my name. And yet on December 10, 1993, World Human Rights Day, Operation Angel, a name thought up by the other organisers, assembled at Brighton pier with two hundred volunteers and fifty-six trucks, ambulances and assorted support vehicles. It was the largest convoy ever to set off from these shores – and it had all been done in three weeks.

The story of how it came together is a remarkable testimony to the resourcefulness and generosity of the people of Britain.

It had begun extremely badly. In fact before we were able to get under way I wasted five precious weeks trying to do things 'through the proper channels'. I had lunch with a man from the Overseas Development Administration, I sent fax after fax to John Major, I tried every political avenue I could think of but each was a dead end.

I did have fun as well, however. I was presented with awards from the Variety Club, the Celebrity Guild and the Ross McWhirter Foundation. Each involved a dinner and dance and

SALLY BECKER

since I had no partner at the time I asked Duncan Stewart to come with me. He was after all an old friend and the first person to provide me with medical supplies for Bosnia; he was also the perfect escort: tall, distinguished, with beautiful manners.

It was an extraordinary feeling to find myself in the middle of a war one minute and the middle of a ballroom floor the next on the arm of a star like Richard Wilson. There was one banquet in the Inner Temple where I found myself surrounded by members of the aristocracy all congratulating me and saying nice things and I remember thinking 'what am I doing here?'

I could not quite bring myself to get decked out in an evening gown and high heels – I had spent so long in my jeans and T-shirt I thought I would look like Dick Emery in drag – and settled instead for a pair of smart black trousers and white evening jacket.

I was also appearing on the odd television programme to talk about Bosnia and Michael Mendoza kept plugging away at the subject on Spectrum Radio but the project was still moving too slowly and on too small a scale.

Then several things happened in quick succession, almost as if they were stepping stones from a dream to its reality. I gave a talk at my local synagogue, through the Adult Jewish Cultural Society, to an audience of maybe two hundred people and they had a whip round at the end: they raised £1,700. It was fantastic. It meant that to begin with I could set up a proper headquarters: until that point I had been covering every surface of my mother's kitchen with papers.

A man called Stewart Weir who had been in the year below me at school turned up offering his services. The first thing he would get me he said was some good secretarial help from the nearby business school and he brought in two women, Justine

128

and Val, who were to prove stalwarts throughout.

Duncan Stewart was a member of the board of a trust set up by his grandfather, Sir Halley Stewart, to provide money for worthy causes and they gave us a thousand pounds. It meant we could buy our first ambulance, a good old Bedford like the one I had driven in Bosnia but in much better condition.

A singer called Gloria Macari and Roger Ferris and Yolanda Beeny, wrote a song called 'Hear the Children' and sang it with a group of children in Brighton. I was so excited when I heard the tape that I rang Neil Morris, the producer of *Good Morning* with Anne Diamond and Nick Owen, and played it to him over the phone. Next day I was on the programme talking about my plan to the show's 'Mr Fixit'. Straightaway he told viewers what I needed: cash, vehicles, volunteers and all the supplies we could get.

At last we had begun to raise people's awareness and things really started moving. A graphic design friend of Duncan's, called Andrew Popkiewicz, worked day and night to produce a leaflet which we had printed by the thousand and sent out to the six co-ordinators Stewart Weir had appointed around the country.

On the leaflet were the words 'An angel rushes in where most of us fear to tread' and a picture of the little boy I had rescued on the second mission with bandages over his injured eyes.

'Surely you can see,' the leaflet said, 'that innocent children must be rescued from their suffering. Through the intervention of people like Sally Becker they have been. Some people cannot help themselves. Muslim, Croat and Serbian children will perish this winter in the freezing conditions of central Bosnia so now she's going back. But Sally Becker and her team of volunteers need all the help they can get.'

It was endorsed by people like Harold Pinter, Lady Antonia Fraser, Chris Eubank, Christopher Timothy, Andrew Bowden MP, Bob Marshall Andrews QC, and Mark Porter, the doctor on Anne and Nick's show who was to come along as the convoy's medical officer. At the bottom was the address of UKJAID, the Jewish Aid and International Development charity, who had agreed to handle our money because we did not have time to get charitable status ourselves.

The response to Operation Angel, as the press had dubbed it, was fantastic. People all over the country began raising money and collecting goods, from little old ladies knitting sweaters to children handing over their pennies in school.

We did not have time to record 'Hear the Children' so *Good Morning* chose another song already on compact disc called 'Remembering Christmas' performed by Bramdean Boys Choir and the BBC made a very moving video to accompany it which raised over £8,000. A *Sunday Mirror* appeal raised £11,000; Sally Line Ferries offered us free passage to France; Nissan loaned us a brand new jeep; Trailblazers gave us citizen band radios and loudspeakers.

An extraordinary man called Mansukh Patel who ran an organisation dedicated to world peace invited Duncan and me to his multi-faith centre in Birmingham, gave us a wonderful vegetarian meal (Duncan found it hard not to smile – I was notorious for my love of junk food), and then marshalled all his followers to prepare hundreds of nutritional food parcels for our journey. His motto was 'every little thing we do, no matter how small, can change the world'.

We had somehow captured the nation's imagination. I think people saw one woman doing what deep down in their hearts they wanted to do but could not because they were afraid or tied up with family commitments and mortgages and jobs. They believed in what I was doing and they believed too that they would see results. It would not be like dropping a coin in a collecting box and wondering what had been done with it. They could follow this as it happened.

There were of course the occasional blunders. One volunteer ambulanceman announced on *Good Morning* that all the one-family aid parcels we had asked people to put together could be dropped off at any ambulance station and as a result every station in the country was inundated with parcels. Unfortunately he had not checked with his bosses first and the telephone did not stop ringing for days as we tried to sort out the misunderstanding and arrange proper collections.

Soon we had over two hundred volunteers. Our stipulation was that they must have some relevant skills and a background that made them used to discipline and not easily frightened or horrified. We were looking for people like nurses, firemen, paramedics, former soldiers. I also did not want anyone who had children. It would defeat the object if I was to save some children but orphan others, unfortunately Stuart was unable to vet them all. Each was asked to contribute one hundred pounds towards their costs: we would provide transport, food and accommodation.

Despite all the donations that were now pouring in – we had almost a million pounds worth of medical supplies and equipment for instance – it seemed at one point that we would not reach our target in time. The ferry from Ancona to Split would be £30,000 alone.

It was then that Duncan stepped in. He had already agreed to join the convoy for which I was enormously grateful. I knew his commitment would be whole-hearted. Now he offered to put up his surgery as surety for a bank loan. In the end we raised all the money we needed but I was touched and honoured by his faith in the operation and in me.

During the time all this was going on, I was also trying to clarify our overall plan. It would be no use having the means if we did not get the end sorted out. The aim was to enter Bosnia and deliver aid to three different sites. I therefore approached the Croats, the Muslims and the Serbs for permission to enter the areas they held. The Croats and the Muslims agreed, the Serbs never replied. We would therefore head for East Mostar, where Muslims were besieged by Croats and Nova Bila hospital where Croats were besieged by Muslims.

I contacted the UN High Commission for Refugees in Zagreb to request protection for the convoy. To my delight their chief of missions, Karen Abuzayd, replied almost immediately and sounded enthusiastic. Would I also, she asked, consider other areas for evacuation which the UN would select but which would be done beneath the umbrella of Operation Angel?

The drawback as far as I was concerned was that the UN wanted its Medivac teams to select all the evacuees, those from East Mostar and Nova Bila as well as those from the areas they would designate. My previous experiences had made me nervous about such procedures and I feared there would be children and others whom I would believe worthy of evacuation but who might not fit the UN's narrow bureaucratic definition. I had no real choice, however: we needed that protection.

There was another problem. We needed hospital beds in Britain and the ODA told me that only those processed by the UN would be accepted. I found myself caught up in a bizarre

Catch 22 situation, for whenever I tried the UN they would say Britain had not agreed to any beds; when I contacted the ODA they would say the UN had not requested any.

The American charity, Veterans for Peace, assured me that they had plenty of beds available in the States, again with the proviso that the evacuees must be authorised by the UN. Veterans for Peace was the organisation which was already caring for some of the children I had brought out earlier including a seventeen-year-old girl who had ridden in my ambulance back in August.

She had written me a wonderful letter:

My Dearest Sally Becker;
My name is Maya Kazazic, the 17 year old girl that you helped to get out of Mostar, on August 26, 1993, having lost my left leg from below the knee, and my right leg was broken in several places, with deep infection had I not got out of Mostar, by your dedicated effort, I doubt that I would be alive today. Words cannot express my respect and gratitude that I have for you, And my Aunt Mayda Paunovic, that came with me as my escort and round-the-clock attendant, also hopes that some day we would have the privilege of once again to meet you. We were brought to the Cumberland Memorial Hospital, in Cumberland, Maryland, U.S.A. where the good fortune that you bestowed upon us, by your dedication, so that when we arrived here our Blessings continued, we were treated just like family by the Doctor, the Nursing Staff, the people of the area, that visited us, doing for us as if we were related to them, we have been repeatedly taken to peoples homes for Dinners, Holidays, Football Games, To the School where I hope to go, we have

so much to be greatful for, that it just bogles our minds. I now have a temporary artificial leg, and am able to get around on my own with a walker, I can't put any weight on my right leg till it heals completely, which shouldn't be too long. We are now in a private home by our selves the house is furnished by the individuals of this support group. We are so happy to be self sufficient, all due to your dedication, thanks ever so much.

I'll close now, with love and respect, and yours truly forever greatfull.

Maya Kazazic, and her Aunt,
Mayda Paunovic, that is equally greatfull to you, thanks ever so much.

If ever I found myself wavering through exhaustion or frustration, I only had to think of the images that letter conjured up and my resolve was strengthened.

By the end of those three weeks we were working twenty-hour days to meet our deadline but we did it. On December 9 more than two hundred people wearing white Operation Angel sweatshirts and baseball caps assembled at the Thistle Hotel in Brighton where they were to stay overnight free of charge. The atmosphere was electric with excitement as I entered the ballroom for the final briefing and was given a standing ovation.

They were a wonderfully varied bunch in both age and background: a man of seventy-plus, a lad of nineteen, nurses, ambulancemen, firemen, two women doctors, a psychologist. There were even my cousins Ashley and David. And of course there was the press. Many would meet us out there but a few, including a BBC crew and a team from Meridian who were making a documentary called *The Angel Returns*, would be travelling with us.

From the platform I explained the picture in Bosnia in as much depth as I could; I described the people and their suffering and what our operation would entail. I told them how gruelling the trip would be, that it would be frightening and harrowing and dangerous and in case anyone still had any doubts we ran twenty minutes of footage from Bosnia which spelled it out in even more graphic terms. I told them that whenever they became bitter or bad-tempered or argumentative, as they surely would, they had to keep sight of our aims. Lastly I told them that if anyone started to spread dissension they would be asked to leave. And I wished us all good luck.

Our transport manager Lawrence Le Carre, an energetic man in his fifties with a mop of bright red hair who had already helped run convoys to Bosnia, explained the driving and emergency procedures in his booming voice and then Duncan briefed them on the medical aspects. He was now in sole charge of this side of the operation since Dr Mark Porter, our medical officer, had suffered an appendicitis and had had to withdraw.

The briefing lasted from 10am until 3pm when the volunteers were free to spend their evenings as they pleased. The mood was a mixture of exhilaration and trepidation. Many had said goodbye to their families, not expecting to return in time for Christmas and perhaps wondering whether they would return at all.

That evening I finally received the UN document I had been waiting for for so long: the list of evacuees. There were more than eighty in East Mostar alone including, to my immense relief, some children. Even more importantly there was the name of the little boy I had left behind in a coma. Perhaps Hafid would have his miracle after all.

There were also several names from Zenica, Tuzla and Sarajevo, all towns in central Bosnia but all predominantly Muslim. There was only one name from Nova Bila hospital. My heart sank. I knew there were many there, including several seriously injured children, who desperately needed to get out. I had been told a few days earlier by the UN that heavy snow had made the roads into central Bosnia impassable. It would therefore be impossible to take the aid trucks in. Instead they would fly Duncan and me up to Sarajevo and carry the evacuees out by air.

I was filled with dismay. Not only would we not be able to deliver aid to the region, we would only be bringing out one person from Nova Bila. I knew the Croats would be enraged: they would think that once again we were reneging on the deal. There was no time to do anything that night but I vowed to change the list as soon as we got to Split.

The next morning the volunteers began to load up and the press asked to do some pictures of us leaving the car park. As we lined up on the street a traffic warden appeared and began working her way along the line, studiously ignoring the whirring cameras and the gales of laughter.

A large crowd of well-wishers had gathered at the pier to see us off. Among them were Gloria and Roger and thirty youngsters who sang 'Hear the Children' as vehicle after vehicle, each painted white and emblazoned with the Operational Angel logo, drew up along the promenade.

'I'll take care of her,' said Duncan to my father.

'More likely she'll take care of you,' retorted my father to the amusement of all around.

I started my engine which was the signal to all the others. My mother stood on the pavement with her sister Jenny, David and Ashley's mother. Tears streamed down her face, her expression a mixture of pride and terror.

'Don't worry, we'll be fine,' I called out and slowly drew away from the kerb. The convoy snaked behind me, blue lights flashing. My heart swelled as I looked at it in my rear view mirror. Operation Angel was under way.

13

AN OGRE, A KNIGHT AND A FEW GREMLINS

We seemed jinxed from the start. A police canteen trailer loaned by the Humberside force jack-knifed on the road and was put out of action. No one was hurt but we had lost our kitchen and Ashley and his friend Nick who were in charge of the catering had to squeeze in with someone else. Then we took a wrong turn and found ourselves heading in the opposite direction to our destination at Ramsgate: apparently someone had put down the wrong road number.

We made it to the port in time and found the coach which had been bought for the journey. The driver had removed most of the seats and spread out mattresses so that drivers could sleep between shifts. We seemed to have far more volunteers than we had orginally planned but I did not have the heart to turn anyone back after all their efforts and I managed to borrow a minibus through Sally Line to accommodate the extras.

On board ship I went to call our representative in France who was trying to trace our free motorway toll passes. As I was returning I overheard a man I vaguely recalled having seen somewhere before in Bosnia giving his opinion in a loud Scottish accent.

'We shouldn't take their route,' he said, swaying slightly. 'I know a far better way. Anyway it's all being done wrong. I don't think we should continue with this woman.'

I pulled on his sleeve. 'This woman would prefer you didn't continue at all,' I said and I heard a cheer behind me.

'First of all you're drunk when drinking during a convoy where everyone is dependent on everyone else is absolutely forbidden. Secondly I also said that anyone trying to stir up trouble would be asked to leave. We are travelling to a war zone for goodness sake. We can't risk anything other than a tight team. You are no longer invited.'

There was silence as everyone waited for his reaction. I knew the incident could make or break my authority with the volunteers.

The man lurched towards me. 'Well, I have to tell you,' he said, 'that firstly I'm not drunk and that secondly I plan to bring out a couple of soldiers who're stuck in central Bosnia so I have to go there.'

I could hardly believe my ears. This idiot was prepared to jeopardise the whole operation by smuggling soldiers through Bosnia.

'You are no longer a part of Operation Angel,' I said coldly. 'You will please remove the stickers from your vehicle and travel separately. I'm sorry but I cannot risk your being connected with us. This is an official evacuation. We are working within UN regulations and I have signed a paper stating I will not make any unauthorised evacuations. As convoy leader I am responsible for everyone else's actions.'

On arrival at Dunkerque I still had to sort out the motorway tolls. It took 'till dawn for a persistent French woman to clear our path. Everyone else slept in their vehicles. Finally we set off and I had the chance to catch up on some sleep while someone else drove the Nissan Patrol. At the first petrol stop the team leaders came up and requested me to go ahead to the next toll to make sure we had free access. It seemed a sensible suggestion at the time but I was to regret it bitterly later.

At the toll we found everything arranged as promised and waited for the convoy. The hours passed and still it did not appear. Just before midnight we decided to go on to a service station down the motorway to try and find out what had happened. After a night of frantic phone calls we had our answer. The convoy had stopped off to unload excess weight: apparently the vehicles were overladen. The Red Cross picked up the aid they had had to leave and it arrived in Bosnia later. Unfortunately the scenes had been filmed by a TV crew and gave the impression that aid was just being dumped. It was to do our reputation immense harm before we got the chance to put the record straight.

Once we knew the convoy was on the road again we headed for the Italian border. When they caught up with us they told us they had arranged a committee among themselves to sort everything out. They had transferred the vital medical supplies to the three biggest trucks which made more room for people to lie down in the other vehicles.

Duncan and I spent hours seeing each group as they arrived, sorting out their grievances and trying to give heart to those who seemed to be losing it. Many were more concerned about their own comfort than about our aims. One man complained that he had not had a hot meal in hours and I found myself reminding him sharply that there were poor souls in Mostar who had not had a hot meal in months.

As Duncan pointed out, some of the volunteers had

package holiday mentalities. It was our fault in the sense that we had not had the time to interview everyone individually to weed out those who had neither the stomach nor the stamina for such an enterprise.

As they ate in the car park – Ashley and others had rigged up some primus stoves – I received a phone call from a man with a Scottish accent. He said he had driven ahead to make sure there would be no hold-ups and that the Italian police needed to speak to me.

I felt exhausted but I set off with Duncan, Lawrence and Mick Fegan, an ex-policeman acting as our security officer. To my dismay I saw that the man at the border post was the loud-mouthed oaf I had 'sacked' on the ferry and I was furious with myself at not having recognised his voice. He was having trouble crossing the border. He had not removed his Operation Angel stickers and was demanding free access through the tolls in our name.

Lawrence became very angry, his outrage fuelled by having been told by one volunteer that this idiot had been boasting about smuggling arms into Bosnia. A scuffle broke out between the two of them until Lawrence landed a punch on the man's nose and he ran off. I kept shaking my head in disbelief. My dream was turning into a nightmare and we had not even reached the war zone yet.

My next worry was an old man who was being cared for by a paramedic. His vehicle had broken down and he had slept in the open waiting for a lift. He was now suffering mild hypothermia and not fit to continue an arduous journey. He would have to be flown back to the UK from Torino.

At last Mick, Duncan and I reached Ancona and checked into the Hotel Jolly, thinking we could perhaps have a well-earned rest. The hotel could not have been less appropriately named. Mike Mendoza rang from Britain: the news was full of reports that our coach had crashed and several people had been seriously hurt.

Duncan paled visibly when I told him the awful news. Eventually we managed to get through to the hospital where the injured had been taken. The coach had been struck from the rear by an Italian lorry going at seventy miles an hour. Thankfully the reports of serious injuries were unfounded: the worst was a whiplash and bruising, the rest were suffering from shock. We arranged for money to be taken from our funds to fly all of them home. The effects of a crash would leave no one in the right state of mind to face the ordeals ahead.

In fact some of those involved in the crash insisted on going on. We all met up again at the quayside and embarked, grateful to find showers and hot food on board. Not everyone could have a cabin so we allocated them to the coach passengers, the elderly and the women, though some of the men refused, insisting on cabins for themselves.

The captain invited me to his table for dinner and we talked about the mission. He even asked me which route he should take and what time I would like him to dock. It felt very strange to be given that sort of control. I was extremely seasick later, caused as much I suppose by exhaustion and stress as by the sea.

We docked next morning in Split harbour in pouring rain. The UN personnel who met us were all very friendly and polite. Duncan and I were to go on to Sarajevo as planned, with the convoy remaining in Makarska until our return when we would start for Mostar. Or so I thought. As I returned from giving a series of interviews before going to Sarajevo, I overheard a UN officer briefing the volunteers.

I marched through the crowd and climbed some scaffolding so everyone could hear me.

'Please ignore everything you have just been told,' I said. 'You will not be going to Mostar tomorrow, you will wait at the hotel until we return, whether it's tonight, tomorrow or the next day. Only then will the Mostar operation take place.

'I have given my word to the Croatian authorities that Mostar will only be evacuated *after* the children are out of Nova Bila. They have made it quite clear that this is to be the way things will happen and we will not jeopardise that. Without their agreement we cannot cross any front line and the operation cannot take place.'

'Suppose something happens to you and you don't make it back,' said one of the women doctors bluntly.

'Then the situation would be out of my hands,' I replied, 'but hopefully the mission would continue without me.'

The UN officer apologised, there had been a misunderstanding he said. Now it was time for us to go. Mark Dowdney from the *Daily Mirror* and Roy the photographer were coming with us as was a freelance cameraman working for Meridian. Everyone gathered round, hugging us and wishing us luck. My cousins Ashley and David had always been fond of Duncan: he had been their GP since they were born. The two of them had had their own narrow escape. They had been on the coach at one stage but had swopped to another vehicle shortly before the accident. The rear seats in which they had been sitting only ten minutes before were crushed on impact. It was bad enough to think of strangers being hurt let alone my own family.

At the UN headquarters in the city we were issued with UNHCR cards which permitted us to travel in their transport and put us under official protection. I smiled at the word consultant written below my photograph. Both Duncan and I had flak jackets but I needed the special plates that fit inside. Duncan had a policeman's bullet-proof vest but was told to leave it behind as he would be issued with a better one in Sarajevo.

As we prepared to cross the tarmac to the plane, however, he was stopped by a soldier.

'You can't go on board without a flak jacket,' he shouted above the roar of the engines. 'It's forbidden under UN rules.'

'He has to come,' I shouted back. 'He's part of this operation and I won't be leaving without him.'

The soldier stared. 'Well, he ain't going nowhere so I suggest you get on board now or stay behind.'

His manner seemed unnecessarily aggressive. I walked up to him. We were almost nose to nose.

'Your boss has caused this problem by taking the flak jacket away. I will not be leaving without him so you can tell your plane to leave empty. And by the way, there's no need to be so damn rude.'

At that moment a BBC cameraman joined us. He had been hoping to board the flight but had not brought his passport with him. He had understood that his UN identity card would be enough, now he was being told it was not, so Duncan was able to ask him for the loan of his flak jacket and we could take off.

We stowed our precious food and medical supplies and sat down beside the Medivac representative, a Frenchwoman called Genevieve who was in charge of this part of our mission. The flight was short and on landing at Sarajevo we raced to unload our belongings as quickly as possible: the tarmac was within the sights of Serbian snipers.

Heads ducked we ran across the tarmac accompanied by the distant sound of gunfire and shelling. The sounds were all too familiar to me but they were new to Duncan and I feared for his safety as he struggled beneath the weight of the heavy boxes. Inside the unlit room where we waited for transport I watched him closely as he chatted to Mark Dowdney who resembled a bank manager; incongruous given the surroundings. Despite his tiredness Duncan stood erect, his hair curled by the drizzle and his eyes an astonishing cornflower blue. He caught my gaze and grinned. I felt my pulse quicken as I realised how important he had become to me.

He seemed unconcerned by the darkness and the danger and his courage made me feel suddenly secure. For the first time since I had become involved in the Bosnia conflict eight months ago I had someone with me on whom I could depend. At that moment he seemed like the original white knight; the only difference was he was wearing a flak jacket instead of shining armour.

Sally being welcomed
back to England by her
two nephews, Joby and
Max, after the harrow-
ing first two evacuations
from East Mostar.

Sally and Duncan
Stewart at the Ross
McWhirter Award cere-
mony.

The volunteers gather in Brighton for the start of Operation Angel.

...ally leading the Operation Angel convoy as it sets off from Brighton.

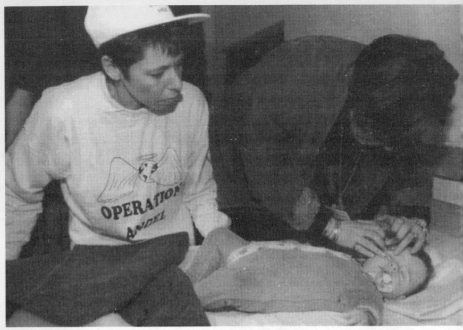

Anton Buhic, a Croatian baby in grave danger of going permanently blind, is examined by a French doctor from the UNHCR at the Field Hospital in Nova Bila.

Sally cuddles a young boy evacuated from East Mostar during Operation Angel. Teddy bear courtesy of Humberside Police.

Sally, holding an armful of
teddy bears, anxiously waits at
Split airport for the first group of
wounded children evacuated
from Tuzla during Operation
Angel.

Sally and Duncan, Brighton
July 1994.

14

THE BABY IN THE MONASTERY

A French officer approached us. The transport that had been due to pick us up had been detained at Serb lines and would not make it by curfew. Instead we were to go to the Holiday Inn for the night.

The road there was pocked with shrapnel holes and the building opposite was burnt and blackened. I could see vague shapes of people running to and fro in the dark to dodge sniper fire. The shadows made everything seem unreal and the interior of the hotel added to the sensation. It was built around an atrium at the top of which was a mass of foliage lit by fairy lights but the top two floors were missing where a shell had struck earlier in the war.

We followed Genevieve through the dim reception area to a candlelit desk where a woman peered at us through a glass panel. We paid for the rooms with credit cards, which made the situation seem even stranger, and climbed the stairs to the fourth floor. They looked like hotel rooms any-where with bathrooms en suite, only here there was no water. They were lit by two lamps and the curtains were drawn tight to prevent light spilling from the window which faced the

Serbian guns. There were already several bullet holes in the glass.

A maid came in to turn down my bed and Duncan presented her with a large bar of hazelnut chocolate as a tip. Her eyes bulged: it was clear she had not tasted chocolate for a very long time.

'She'll probably be able to sell it on the black market for food,' I told him.

'She'll probably be able to buy a house with it,' he replied.

'I should have got a discount on this room,' I said. 'Eighty pounds a night seems a high price to pay to face the most dangerous side.'

We switched on the television and CNN appeared. It seemed extraordinary to be able to watch satellite TV in such surroundings. Duncan flicked over to a Western and turned off the sound.

'Why did you do that?' I asked.

'We've got the real thing outside,' he said and we both laughed. We needed to make silly jokes.

The room was freezing cold for there was snow outside and no heat within. I wanted to huddle beneath the covers of the bed but first we needed to eat.

'I'll go and scout around for some food,' Duncan said and went out into the corridor. I saw he had forgotten his torch. Ten minutes after he left the lights went out and the darkness was total. I sat half sick with anxiety trying to picture him wandering around in that blackness. After what seemed like ages someone touched my arm. I reeled with shock. It was Duncan. He had managed to find the way back using his fingers to trace the numbers on the doors.

'God, you scared me,' I cried in relief.

'I've found the dining room,' he said proudly. 'Would you care to join me for dinner.'

I took his arm and using the torch we picked our way down the stairs. I gasped as we entered the dining room. Before us was the most extraordinary sight. Tables were laid with soft white cloths and gleaming cutlery and there was a warm glow from the subdued lighting. Waiters in tangerine suits and starched white shirts and black bow ties bustled between the tables. There was a quiet buzz of conversation. Most of the tables were full but Mark Dowdney had saved us a place. It was as if we had been transported from a war zone to a top class hotel in Mayfair.

The meal however was a stark reminder that we were a long way from Mayfair. The bread was freshly baked and soft but the meat had an odd sweet flavour and I almost choked when Duncan suggested it might be horse flesh. The wine cost forty dollars and tasted foul, the coffee was ten dollars a cup. Still, we were eating in a city where people had stripped bark off trees to fill their empty bellies. Most of our fellow diners were journalists and UN personnel. The talk was that the hotel paid protection money to the Serbs in order to continue in business. I could well believe it.

Afterwards we made our way back through the gloom to my room to discuss our arrangements for the morning. It was so cold I snuggled up to Duncan for warmth. Beyond the taint of my cigarettes he had a fresh soapy smell and I felt immensely comforted as his arms enveloped me. Life seemed so tenuous in this uncertain place.

I knew I was falling in love and I wished fervently that if anything should happen it would be to me, not him. I knew too how precious his life was to so many others and at that moment

I regretted ever having asked him to join me on this dangerous journey.

I voiced my fears. If I was ever to be seriously injured I told him, he must not endanger himself to help me.

'Promise me,' I whispered.

'I can't,' he replied. 'I can't promise to walk away and let you die.'

'Please,' I pleaded, 'Tell me you won't take a risk with your own life.'

He saw how much the answer meant to me and he promised. I knew he was too unselfish ever to abide by it but it gave me the reassurance I needed. He left and I got into bed. It was icy but I had no trouble sleeping. The fears, the dangers, the sadness suddenly seemed far away.

Next morning we were driven to the UN base in Kiseljak, formerly a ski resort hotel with panoramic views, and given our itinerary which included visits to a hospital and an orphanage on our evacuation list. Nova Bila hospital was not included: the only man there who had passed the Medivac assessment did not now wish to leave. But we must go there, I insisted, if only to take the small amount of medical aid we had brought with us and to see the situation for ourselves.

Nova Bila, a few kilometres from the British base at Vitez, was surrounded by BIH forces and the old converted monastery was now a hospital for the wounded as well as the sick. There were few beds and most patients lay stretched out in pews. The main ward was also the chapel and the doctor in charge was a Franciscan monk. He had been expecting me, he said, for a long time.

As we spoke there was a sudden commotion and a man with a bullet lodged in his head was rushed into the one operating theatre. The cameras began to whirr but to our surprise no one attempted to stop them. In fact, even as the man died, one of the doctors, blood still dripping from his hands, twisted the poor wretch's face towards the camera to show the world the full horror of their situation. Duncan turned away, appalled.

We toured the hospital and listened to the case histories: soldiers wounded in the fighting, limbless, eyeless, sometimes both; women, young and old, maimed by shrapnel; children, eight of them all under twelve, one with a leg missing, another with both arms gone, a third blind, a fourth horribly burned. Someone put a baby in my arms. Anton was eight months old and he was going blind; no one knew why. They had no facilities to run any test. As I held his small, limp body his mother broke into sobs beside me.

Someone translated: 'My husband has been killed. I am alone with my baby and my little girl. Please help us, please take us out of here so that my baby can be treated, so my children can live.'

I bent to try and comfort her but her little daughter struck out at me with her tiny fists. All she knew was that my presence there had made her mother cry. Frustration and rage welled up inside me. Why could these children not be evacuated?

Genevieve rounded on me.

'You promised beds,' she cried. 'But your country knows nothing about it. This child cannot be evacuated to the places we have available. This child is not dying. There are others in much more serious need.'

'He's going blind,' I said, 'doesn't that count? Doesn't he deserve the chance of a normal life?'

'There aren't places for these cases. Your government hasn't any places because you didn't get any arranged.'

I was outraged by her accusations. After all my attempts to persuade the government to help, after all the letters I had written to John Major, to Margaret Thatcher, to the ODA, to the Home Office, to anyone I could think of. I had tried every tactic I knew and so had my friends with their political contacts. And always the answer had come back: the beds must be applied for by Medivac, by the United Nations, by the International Office of Migration.

On impulse I spun round to face the camera, the child still in my arms.

'Please don't leave children like this here to die,' I pleaded. 'John Major, I beg you, please help them. Give us the beds so they can be saved.'

In another room I tried to explain to the hospital staff that I *was* trying to evacuate their wounded but was being prevented from doing so. They told me that Genevieve had not been near the hospital in weeks. The one man who had been put on the list of evacuees did not want to leave without the rest. To make matters even more confusing I learned that another convoy run by Dr Slobodan Lang, a Jewish Croat from Zagreb, was on its way, as was one arranged by the Muslims to Zenica. So much for the roads being impassable.

None of it made sense and it was impossible to decide who was speaking the truth. All I could do was promise them I would continue to push for an evacuation; if it did not happen I would come back and do it myself.

After this meeting Duncan and I were taken to the maternity ward and watched enchanted as a jolly midwife placed a newborn baby in the arms of its young mother. There was only one obstetrics bed for the hundreds of women in the area and this was the one hundred and tenth baby to be born in it. We felt immensely cheered by the mother's joy and the midwife's obvious delight in her work. Despite the horrors of the war outside the door, despite our own confusions and fears, there was still new life to be cherished.

Back at the APCs, however, the frustrations soon resurfaced. Genevieve was giving a television interview and lambasting me for misleading the UN. I felt suddenly weary at the thought of having to defend myself all over again and turned away. The Franciscan begged one of our Operation Angel T-shirts and gave us gifts in return: a black and white print for me inscribed with thanks to the Angel of Nova Bila and a watercolour for Duncan of an angel holding a priest. I was touched and saddened: despite all my efforts I had so far been unable to help them at all.

As we travelled away from Nova Bila our vehicle was caught in crossfire, and as the bullets ricocheted off the armour plating, we were grateful for the skill of the soldier driving the APC in which we sat.

Our next stop was Vitez where our host, Tohler, was a Coldstream Guards major of impeccable manners and military bearing who briefed us on the local position. All sides passed on information knowing it would not be released to the others with the result that not a soldier or a weapon moved without UNPROFOR knowing about it. The major was informative and amusing and despite the set-backs of the day we found ourselves still able to laugh.

He told us for instance about an arms factory, which hadn't yet been hit because it was coveted by all sides, that was situated beside a marmalade manufacturers. If anyone did blow it up, said Duncan to a chorus of groans, it could create a very sticky situation.

That evening we ate better than we had in days and spent a pleasant couple of hours watching the officers rehearse their Christmas show. Afterwards I was invited to spend the night in Colonel Peter Williams' house. The gallant colonel led the way himself, stamping a path through the thick mud which was the bane of every soldier's life so that I could literally follow in his footsteps.

I slept well that night despite all the conflicting information whirling around in my brain and woke refreshed. I had a hot bath, a change of clothes and coffee from a young soldier who would insist on calling me 'Ma'am' despite my protestations. Duncan had spent the night in the barracks where he too had slept soundly alongside the press men and the soldiers.

We had great sympathy for the soldiers. They were a brave bunch and I was proud they were British. For some it was their first experience in the field and their already difficult job was made even more so by the increasing desperation of the local people. So bad had it become that they sometimes encouraged their children to run in front of the aid trucks, forcing them to stop. As the vehicles braked other youngsters would clamber aboard and throw down as many packages as they could. To add to the danger they lived beneath the threat of the large guns situated in the surrounding hills.

Genevieve rejoined us as we waited for our return transport and we clashed almost immediately. I was angry that she had criticised me to the media; she accused me of being a liar, almost spitting the word from a mouth twisted with fury. What's more, she said, I had exploited a child on camera.

I was incensed. 'If holding that baby up to the camera will embarrass the Prime Minister into saving its life, then yes, I exploited it,' I said.

Later as we drove back, a voice came over the driver's radio informing us that Britain had offered sixteen beds as a result of my plea. We cheered in the back and Duncan squeezed my hand. Genevieve was travelling in another vehicle so I was unable to watch her expression.

Back in Kiseljak we were told that there were no more flights out of Sarajevo that day but that the Mostar evacuation would take place the next morning as planned. I felt shocked and extremely concerned. I was holding all the permissions necessary to cross the line. How were my volunteers to get through the checkpoints? They probably would not go, said the officer who had delivered this message; instead the evacuation would be done by the UN in their armoured vehicles.

That made sense on one level – the patients would be safer – but I could not see how they could accommodate eighty-odd people unless they had suddenly acquired unlimited transport. It also meant of course that no aid would get in. I could not see why they had bothered to team up with me at all if neither I nor my volunteers were needed.

The more I thought about it the less likelihood I could see of the evacuation taking place at all. The permission had been granted to me personally: East Mostar was the quid pro quo for Nova Bila and Nova Bila had not yet happened. My worst fears were realised when the officer was called to the phone. He returned looking worried.

'The Croats have called off the Mostar evacuation,' he said despondently.

'Get me back there,' I urged. 'I'll speak to them, they'll let me go, I'm sure they will.'

He looked at me strangely. Who on earth was this mad woman who thought she could change the mind of a general?

15

THE DREAM BECOMES A NIGHTMARE

There was a flight out of Sarajevo to Split after all. We rushed through check-in where a sign proclaimed 'Maybe Airlines', a darkly humorous reference to the number of planes that either didn't make it or never left the ground, and out on to the tarmac. It was first come, first served. I sighed with relief as the plane rose into the air. I was frantic to get back and finish the job I had come to do. I must get to Ivan or he would believe I had betrayed him.

Lawrence and Mick were among those meeting us at Split. They looked worn out and with good reason as I was to discover. The UN had taken over the convoy. I was so furious I could hardly speak let alone drive and Lawrence took the wheel of the Nissan as we headed towards Makarska to find the officer, named Major Need, liaising between the UN and my convoy.

The hotel looked superb nestling among trees a few yards from the sea but there was no time to explore.

'Where is everyone?' I yelled at the UN officer as he sat in the office.

'All your vehicles are in Metkovic,' he said calmly.

'What the hell are they doing there?' I demanded. 'My instructions were very clear. Everyone should stay here until I got back. They should only leave the hotel to deliver aid to local refugee camps where it's safe.'

'They had to go to Metkovic to unload the aid into the UN warehouse and wait there until the evacuees were brought out of East Mostar. That should have been tomorrow but was stopped at the last minute,' came the reply.

'How dare you commandeer my convoy, how dare you hijack my aid,' I cried in anger. 'You had no right.'

'I've told you,' he sighed. 'We thought you wouldn't be coming back so we decided to go ahead without you.'

'Why didn't you call Vitez last night?' I demanded. 'Why have you unloaded all my aid?'

He shifted slightly. 'The aid can't be delivered to Mostar. Your people aren't needed for that leg of the journey. Anyway we took some aid in yesterday and your firemen helped deliver it.'

'Bullshit,' I shouted and marched from the office.

The major followed me, trying to explain, but I was beyond listening.

'Get my people back tonight,' I said very quietly. 'Arrange it now. I want them here in this hotel. I will arrange a meeting with Bagaric and I hope to God you people haven't screwed up the whole operation. And make sure that the million pounds worth of medical supplies we brought with us are released from the warehouse in time for our journey to Mostar.'

'I'll call them now,' he said. 'They'll be back tonight. And by the way, don't say "you people". I am a royal marine. I liaise between you and the UN. That is all. I do not make the decisions.'

Despite my anger I liked him. He was a straightforward man caught in the uncomfortable position of go-between. I called Ivan but was told he did not want to see me, he was too busy. He was also, the translator added, very disappointed in me. The UN had asked for the mission to be delayed until the following Tuesday and his people had agreed.

I was aghast at this latest news. The UN knew very well that the volunteers were scheduled to leave on the Sunday evening ferry. We could not afford any extra accommodation or food or the costs of cancelling the ferry. Even if we could, the professionals among us like firemen and paramedics would be expected back at their jobs. It would be unthinkable to leave the emergency services back home short-staffed over Christmas.

Ivan would still not come to the phone but he did agree to discuss the situation with his associates. I went upstairs with Duncan to await the call. The major returned just as the phone rang and waited while I spoke.

'The UN have lied to me,' I told Ivan. 'They say it was your people who insisted on the delay.' Finally I got him to agree to meet me face to face; he would come over later that evening.

As I replaced the receiver I noticed that the major was red in the face with suppressed anger.

'How dare you call us liars,' he exploded. 'I've had enough of this whole situation.' He turned on his heel and left the room.

Now it was the turn of Duncan, cool, calm, collected Duncan, to lose his temper and it shocked me far more.

'For goodness sake, Sally,' he shouted. 'You've blown the whole operation now. Why on earth can't you be more diplomatic?'

I felt as though I had been hit in the stomach. This was the one person who was aware of everything that had happened, the one person I expected to side with me.

'Diplomatic?' I cried. 'Diplomatic? It wasn't diplomacy that enabled me to cross front lines and bring children out. It wasn't being diplomatic that helped me escape the bullets caused by UN inefficiency.'

'I'm going downstairs to see if I can stop that man leaving,' said Duncan. 'I'll apologise to him, though it's probably too late.'

He strode from the room and I ran after him, calling down the corridor.

'He won't leave. They needed me, don't you see? I was their human passport. I got the permission to do what they could not do alone. Not only that, they want the publicity. Why do you think they encouraged the press to be here for the Mostar operation? You don't understand, do you? It should be them apologising to me. They used me for their own ends. They've taken all our supplies, conned the volunteers into thinking I wouldn't be back, that I'd let them down . . .'

I was still raging when the lift doors closed. I cooled down as I showered and changed for my meeting with Ivan. Duncan returned to the room.

'The major's still here,' he said. 'He's not leaving but he said it was a close thing. He's never lost his temper before.'

I went downstairs to find the officer and apologise.

'Look,' I said, 'I'm sorry for what I said to you. I understand that you aren't to blame but it all seems so strange. Please tell me what's going on.'

He told me. My volunteers had received instructions, from me they thought, to move everything to the warehouse. My vehicles were invaluable to the mission because they would be

158

used to transfer the patients from Metkovic to Split once the UN had actually brought them across the line. A large amount of supplies had been delivered to various refugee camps in the area by the volunteers who had been tremendously moved by what they had seen and felt they had done a worthwhile job. The medical supplies would be sorted out shortly.

Ivan and his interpreter arrived and we spent an hour trying to clarify the position. He was adamant the UN had requested Tuesday as the day for the mission. I was beyond caring who had asked for what. What I wanted him to do was rearrange things so that we could do it on the following day, the Saturday.

He shook his head. It would be impossible to arrange a ceasefire at such short notice; besides, he reminded me, I had still not evacuated Nova Bila hospital.

'But the only man who made the list did not want to leave,' I said.

'He's out,' said Ivan. 'His brother arranged a helicopter and flew in to fetch him last night.'

How astonishing – and how admirable – I thought but Ivan pressed on. He was more concerned now he said about the other convoy which was on its way to them under the 'white roads' system. This was the brainchild of Dr Slobodan Lang who was trying to open up routes to all the hospitals in the country to bring aid and medical staff in and take patients out. I had played a small part in the attempts to set up the project when I was back in London by passing messages between the Bosnian Embassy and the Croats.

Now though the convoy was being held up by Muslims; one man had already been killed and the drivers were being held hostage. Ivan wanted the convoy released. My head spun. It was all becoming more confused and complicated by the hour. How could I salvage something out of this mess?

I leaned forward and held Ivan's gaze.

'All I can offer you is this,' I said. 'You allow me to take the convoy to East Mostar to evacuate the children and afterwards I will go back to Nova Bila and stay there as a protest until the convoy arrives. I'll stay for as long as it takes.'

He looked thoughtful as my words were translated. He knew the press would follow my movements which would put pressure on those holding the drivers hostage. Eventually he gathered his papers together and stood up.

'I cannot promise anything,' he said. 'You have let us down. But I am Ivan Bagaric and I want to save lives. I will do what I can for Sally Becker, Angel of Mostar and Nova Bila.'

I noticed his little finger was bare.

'Where's your ring?' I asked.

'I will wear it when I no longer feel you have betrayed me,' he said and I saw the bitter disappointment in his eyes.

The convoy returned empty, its supplies unloaded. The volunteers however were full of hostility. One older man with a grey beard voiced his thoughts angrily.

'You must never organise anything like this again. You have put people's lives at risk. We believed in you and we followed you and you let us down. I have been saying this behind your back as have a lot of others so I think it only fair that I say it to your face.'

The ever-present cameras began to turn.

'You're not just saying it to me, you're saying it to the whole of Britain,' I said and pointed to the TV crew. The man made a move towards them.

'No,' I cried, 'leave them. I want to defend myself. I am an artist, not a professional convoy leader. I never professed to be an expert.

'I said what I wanted to do here and I invited people to join me. I figured that grown men and women, especially professionals, would act appropriately on such an operation. I didn't expect to hear so much whining and complaining wherever there was any discomfort or set-backs. I never said there would be no problems. This is a war, for God's sake.'

'People could have died in that coach crash,' came the accusation.

'The crash was an act of God,' I said. 'I could hardly have prevented a stray lorry hitting the rear of a coach. As for the rest of it, you were told to stay here in this nice safe hotel while Duncan and I went up to central Bosnia. We have spent our time watching a man die in front of our eyes, listening to a mother weep for her child.

'This convoy was my dream. The day it all came together was the happiest day of my life. It's still my dream. We're here to help the wounded and the dying. Let's focus on what we came for.'

As I walked away, a group of volunteers came over to me.

'Sally,' a woman said softly, 'he is not speaking for all of us. We joined because we believed in you and we still believe in you. You have our undivided loyalty, no matter what.'

A lump rose in my throat.

'Thanks guys,' I murmured and turned away so they would not see the tears in my eyes.

16

MISSION ACCOMPLISHED

That night we attended a briefing given by Major Need on behalf of the UN. They had decided to go ahead with the evacuation of East Mostar despite the lack of official permission: they would use a slot that had already been arranged for aid trucks.

'You surely can't mean to defy the Croats and risk the lives of the patients,' I said. 'They'll stop you at the first checkpoint.'

'That's where you come in,' came the reply. 'You'll be up front with all the TV cameras and you'll do what you're good at. You'll use the media to embarrass the Croats into letting us pass.'

'Oh no, I won't,' I said, appalled at the idea. 'I can get this mission arranged without having to blackmail them on world television.'

The next day we were invited to Split airport to see the arrival of the first casualties from Tuzla and Zenica who had been evacuated under the auspices of Operation Angel. Including those being flown in from Sarajevo, more than fifty people would be taken from Split to Ancona that day.

As we watched the Sea Kings land with their precious cargo,

all the frustration and anger and the harsh words were forgotten. A UN officer ran with us to the aircraft, our arms filled with soft toys and baseball caps for the children.

As I stood at the entrance people called out and held up their children. I was not the only one profoundly moved by the moment, it was about saving ordinary people and from the expressions on the faces of the volunteers watching from the terrace above I could tell this made it all worthwhile for them.

There was a message from Ivan back at the hotel. He wanted me to fax the President's office with my offer to go to Nova Bila. I knew then that everything would be all right and that night the UN came to announce that the mission would take place at four the next morning.

I asked if I could take the medical supplies in but the answer was no: we would be travelling in an armoured personnel carrier along with six others. Why was everything such a struggle?

'I cannot go to East Mostar hospital and not take in the things we have brought all the way from England,' I protested. 'Those supplies are vital to the people trapped in that city.'

'Well,' the UN official pondered. 'I suppose you could take in the supplies in your own vehicle but that would be extremely dangerous and unnecessary.'

'It's hardly unnecessary,' I said. 'We have a million pounds worth. People worked incredibly hard to collect them.'

He sighed with annoyance but conceded the point. 'We'll have the supplies delivered to you at the last checkpoint and sandwich your car between armoured vehicles for safety.'

That night everyone went to bed early: almost all the volunteers would be needed at Metkovic to receive the patients. I was just saying goodnight to Duncan when Mick appeared at the door. 'Take care of yourself, please' he said, hugging me. His eyes filled with tears as he walked away. Duncan then told me that he would be joining me in my vehicle but I refused adamantly. No way would I allow him to take more risks than were strictly necessary. It was bad enough that I had no choice about driving in an unarmoured vehicle but there was no point in us both being easy targets.

I tried desperately hard to get some sleep but the truth was I felt very frightened about driving across the line again. I had done it three times under fire and I had been lucky each time. Somehow I did not feel lucky anymore.

We left Makarska at three thirty without so much as a cup of coffee. It was still dark when we pulled up at the UN warehouse in Metkovic two hours later and I was given the steel plates for my flak jacket. Our first rendezvous was the checkpoint between Metkovic and Mostar manned by Croatian militia. Ahead of me were several armoured personnel carriers driven by Spanish UNPROFOR officers. Duncan had to leave me there: he was to travel in one of the armoured jeeps. His driver was Jerry Hulme who greeted me with a bemused expression.

The same UN official from the night before asked me for my UNHCR identity card and explained that I was no longer under their protection. 'We have no responsibility to you in an unarmoured vehicle.' I would now have to drive in an exposed position at the back of the convoy.

I was not too concerned about that. I had never had their protection in Mostar before, why should it make a difference now? As we waited for the Croats to let us through Duncan returned to my Nissan. I tried to hide the terror I was feeling but my hands were trembling. An engine was started: it was the signal for us to move out. Duncan leaned through the window and kissed me gently for luck. I watched him walk away, a tall slim figure silhouetted against the dawn.

I turned on my tape as I drove and heard Gloria Macari's clear tones:

'Can you hear them? Do you care? Listen to the children, crying out there. All the pain and suffering. They never asked to play our games. They wander blindly through the streets wondering what's happening. Through the tears you see the pain, will they ever smile again? So stop, see how the world could be, be free or is it too late to be loving.'

Then the chorus of children's voices:

'We are the children, listen to our voices. We are the future, all our dreams are dying. We are the gift of life, we have the right to survive. Oh mankind, please don't take away our world.'

As I listened and drove towards the now familiar front line I saw the faces of the children whose lives I had touched, those I had helped save, those I had had to leave behind. I pictured the blank eyes of Anton, the baby in the monastery, and I vowed I would come back for him.

I drove on through the city, the journalists' armoured landrover ahead of me. A BIH soldier stepped out and we pulled up. He directed us round the corner to the now familiar war office. The convoy had gone on ahead and I wondered what was happening. We were all asked to go up to the office on the first floor. As we approached the stairs I saw a man I had met at the hospital.

'I want to thank you,' he said and introduced me to his wife. 'You saved our daughter. You remember? She had a serious spinal injury and needed an operation. Because of your insistence the UN finally came to take her out. She is safe and well. We will always be in your debt.'

I smiled and followed the soldier into an office. An imposing looking man directed us to seats around a large table. On the wall was a mural of the Mostar bridge. It had survived nearly five hundred years of wars and earthquakes and other disasters only to fall to the Croat artillery. A symbol of civic pride and tradition, its loss had been a terrible blow to the morale of the citizens.

'You cannot enter the city,' the man declared.

'Why ever not?' I asked.

'Because none of you is on the UNPROFOR list which we now insist on having twenty-four hours in advance.'

'We must be on it,' I said. 'Surely my name is there. It's my Operation.'

The interpreter looked terribly ill: he was shaking and seemed feverish. He repeated my words and they both looked confused.

'What do you mean, your Operation?' he asked.

'Operation Angel is the name of my evacuation,' I explained.

'I know that is the title of this mission,' he replied, 'but I don't understand what you have to do with it.'

'She *is* Operation Angel,' said Mark Downdy. 'It was her idea.'

The men withdrew and we waited for nearly an hour. I remembered then that the medical supplies had not been given to me after all. All I had in the Nissan were several food parcels, blankets and a few clothes. I also had Duncan's torch for Hafid, a Christmas cake and most of the other items he had requested. I wondered how on earth I was going to get them to him under the circumstances.

Slowly it dawned on me what was happening. The UN had made sure our names were not forwarded: by keeping myself and the press away from the hospital the credit for the evacuation would be theirs alone. I was certain that they had their own cameramen with them. It was all madness.

I wasn't at all concerned about the media being allowed to cover my visit but I desperately wanted to see Hafid and the others. I wanted to be able to give some hope to those who would not make it on this trip. If they could see I had kept my word and returned this time, they would know I would come back again. I felt sick at heart. The press were told they could leave but I was to remain. As I sat gazing out of the window I suddenly spotted Duncan in the street below.

'We've been held here,' I called. 'Please don't let them go without me.' I couldn't face being trapped in East Mostar again.

A while later a man came to take me downstairs.

'There has been a misunderstanding,' he apologised. 'We know now who you are. You are very welcome to go to the hospital if you wish.'

I walked out into the street to find Duncan in deep conversation with Jerry Hulme.

'This is the dirtiest trick I have ever seen,' I said to Jerry who stood there smiling calmly. 'It's pathetic. You let me drive in without protection, telling me it's the only way I can get supplies in, then you don't give me the supplies. And all the time you knew I wouldn't even make it to the hospital.'

An ITN camera began to whirr and Jerry addressed me as though trying to calm an hysteric.

'Now, now, Sally. You're being paranoid again. If you want to go to the hospital so badly, I'll take you myself. Unfortunately I'm afraid a man was shot at the entrance by a sniper. If you don't mind the fact that they'll probably be more concerned with that than with welcoming you, we'll go.'

I felt devastated. Of course I could not go rushing into the hospital while they were recovering their dead and I said so.

'Then we'll leave now,' he said. 'The patients are all in the vehicles, all forty-four of them.'

'It was supposed to be eighty-four,' I said miserably.

'Unfortunately many of those on your list failed to reach the hospital this morning.'

'Can't you find them?'

'No, they're all over the place. The shelling prevented them from leaving their homes last night.'

There seemed nothing more I could do. Duncan put his arm around me and I crumpled against him, sobbing broken-heartedly. I had no more fight left in me.

'We have to go now,' said Jerry and strode towards his vehicle. Duncan offered to drive with me but I declined. I was past caring by then. What did it matter if a sniper got me. I kept thinking of Hafid, so near, yet so far. Suddenly I recognised a mop of red hair. It was Tim, the young American Volunteer. He ran over and hugged me.

'What are you doing here?' I asked him.

'We've got permission for a mobile hospital to cross the line,' he said happily. 'It should be here any day.'

'Tim, please can you get these things to Hafid and the others at the hospital?' I asked urgently. The convoy was beginning to pull away. Quickly I heaved the boxes from the back of the Nissan: food, chocolates, coffee, beer, vitamins, sweatshirts, cheese. We piled it high in the road as Tim called to his friends to help. I scribbled a note to Hafid sending my apologies and love and the wish that we would meet again when the war was over. I handed it to Tim along with the Christmas cake and the torch.

168

'I have to go now, take care,' I called as I climbed into the driver's seat and turned the engine.

My flak jacket still lay on the seat beside me and I was tempted to throw it out too but I knew I had no money to pay for its loss. As I drove along the muddy track up the side of the hill the wheels skidded: I had forgotten how to use a four wheel drive. Just as I was sure I would spin over the edge they gripped the ground and I had control again. I was lucky not to hit the waist-high mines obstructing the road.

I stopped at the Croat checkpoint once we were out of the war zone, still fearful that they might not allow the evacuees through. I still had my old documents and hoped they might help if a problem arose. Jerry saw I had stopped and reversed. He and Duncan got out.

'Come on,' said Duncan sharply. 'I'll drive.' He obviously thought I had lost control.

'I'm fine,' I said. 'I'm waiting for our patients. You're welcome to join me.'

Duncan climbed into the vehicle as Jerry opened my door.

'You can't stay here,' he said. 'We're going back to Metkovic.'

'You go,' I told him. 'We'll be along with the others.'

He hesitated for a moment. Then he said 'Stay if you must but I wish you'd stop being paranoid. Operation Angel was a UN thing. Oh you helped of course. Without your fifty ambulances we couldn't have carried so many people. But the rest of it wasn't to do with you.'

I looked at him hard. Then I laughed. 'And I suppose the name of the operation was just coincidental.'

Once the armoured personnel carriers had passed through the checkpoint we drove towards Metkovic and Duncan told me what he had seen at the hospital while I was being held at the war office. He had known what to expect from my descriptions but he was still shocked by the horrors in that basement. He told me how he had seen some of the children, tagged with their names as they waited to be evacuated. One of those he described was the little boy Hafid had saved and who was still in a coma. Whilst they were gathering outside the UN stretchers went back and forth relaying patients, the UN cameras whirring throughout. One UN soldier standing by his side was becoming increasingly agitated, explaining to Duncan how this would be a perfect opportunity for the Croats to shell the hospital.

Back at Metkovic an incredible sight greeted our eyes. All the ambulances were ranged in a large circle like a wagon train camp in a Western and beside each was one of our medical teams. Those patients who could walk were escorted gently into the ambulances, those who could not were borne in on stretchers. There were tears on the faces of the volunteers as they helped carry the children inside. I heard a young ambulance woman talking to a television interviewer.

'Yes,' she said, 'seeing this today makes it all worthwhile.'

'Would you do it again?' he asked.

'Yes,' she answered, 'but without Sally Becker, the woman was never there.'

'But without Sally Becker,' said the interviewer, 'it would never have happened.'

Just then I saw Major Need, the liaison officer, and went over to say goodbye. To my surprise he reached out and hugged me warmly. I stepped back and looked into his eyes where I saw a mixture of admiration and sheer relief at the fact that I was leaving. It was a sweet moment of real human contact beneath the usual bureaucratic mask.

We headed back along the lovely Croatian coast with night falling and all the blue lights on the ambulances flashing through the dusk. Duncan and I drove at the head of the long line of vehicles and I watched them snaking out behind us. Inside each one were people whose wishes had at last come true. I thought it was the most beautiful sight I had ever seen.

At Split airport the patients were transferred on to the waiting planes. I heard a man call out 'Sally gave me her blood.' I do not know who he was or how he knew the blood was mine but it was an immensely heartening thing to hear.

I was free to go home myself now – a message had been sent that the 'white roads' convoy had at last reached Nova Bila – and we sat on the floor of the plane surrounded by the evacuees. At Ancona there was one last job to do: transfer those six children and ten adults who had been given beds in Britain into the care of the paediatric team who were to look after them. Lawrence was driving the Nissan back to England and the rest of the volunteers were going to return in small groups to try and avoid the sort of problems that we had experienced on the way out.

At last we were able to relax on board the flight home. I chatted to all the patients and their relatives and slipped each of the adults fifty pounds so they would not arrive penniless. Those children who could sit up enjoyed themselves enormously and tucked into shepherd's pie and cake; some even managed a visit to the flight deck.

We landed at Birmingham to a media scrum. At the press conference a journalist called out: 'Sally, the United Nations say they could have done this without you.'

'Then why the bloody hell didn't they?' I said.

PART FOUR

Nova Bila

17

PATIENCE IS A VIRTUE

The press was cruel: 'Angel Has Wings Clipped', said one headline; 'Tarnished Halo', said another. The public it seems wants its heroes and heroines to have feet of clay. But I was beyond caring. It did not matter to me what they said. All that mattered was that despite all the set-backs, the bitter quarrels, the tangle of truths and untruths, the confusions of the hour, we had come through. Nearly a hundred people – ninety-eight to be precise – were safe at last. For them at least the war was over.

It was not over for me though. Operation Angel had taught me some harsh lessons; if I was to do it all over again I would do it differently. I would have far fewer volunteers, just a tight-knit team with each member thoroughly vetted, and I would want to be clear about the UN's exact role right from the beginning.

I wanted to do one more big operation, this time by air, taking supplies in to central Bosnia and bringing evacuees out. I telephoned the United Nations headquarters in Zagreb several times and wrote to the chief of missions requesting their assistance. At the end of January the reply came back: the UN would not be able to assist me.

I tried other avenues. Paddy Ashdown, leader of the Liberal Democrats was the only politician to reply. He had written, he said, to the Defence Secretary Malcolm Rifkind and General Sir Michael Rose who was now in charge of the UN in Bosnia asking for their help on my behalf. He could not be involved further but I was immensely encouraged by his words.

I also contacted Dr Lang, the man who had instigated the 'white roads' convoys. He was putting another one together, this time with the extraordinary combination of both Muslim and Croat drivers, and hoped to reach such places as Zenica, Sarajevo and Nova Bila hospital.

Nova Bila! The name was engraved on my heart. It was the last promise I had to keep. Baby Anton and his unseeing eyes haunted my dreams. He represented everything I had promised the Croats and had not been able to deliver.

I had heard nothing from Ivan Bagaric since my return despite a stream of faxes and telephone calls and I knew he believed I had let him down. That mattered very much indeed to me. I thought of him as my friend and I wanted to prove that I had not used him, that I would keep my word and do for his people what he had allowed me to do for his enemy.

Dr Lang said I was welcome to join his convoy. Within five days I was ready to leave. I had five hundred pounds of my own money and a supply of warm clothes. Just before I left, Duncan took me away for our first weekend together. We stayed in country hotels and strolled round ancient churches and beautiful villages but the knowledge that I would be flying into the unknown again when the weekend was over cast a pall over the precious hours.

On the Sunday evening he drove me to Heathrow where several journalists and television crews were waiting. It was awkward trying to say goodbye to each other in front of them. Duncan pulled me aside.

'I love you Miss Becker,' he whispered.

'I love you too Doc,' I said.

Tears pricked my eyes as I watched him waving at me through passport control. Parting was bad enough; parting to return to Bosnia where a bullet might have my name on it seemed almost unbearable.

The tension over there this time was heightened by the decision to use air strikes against the Serbs if they did not lift the siege of Sarajevo. The countdown was about to begin: they had one last chance to pull back their forces and hand over their heavy artillery. The plane to Split was packed with soldiers and UN personnel and the airport even more teeming than usual.

Finally I got hold of my baggage and a taxi to take me to the Hotel Split where I was to stay until arrangements could be finalised. The hotel had few guests apart from EEC monitors but was packed with refugees. I spent the first couple of days in my room making phone calls to the Ministry of Defence in Herzegovina, waiting for news from Dr Lang and following the daily developments on CNN.

I am a restless person at the best of times and the waiting seemed intolerable. I had already wasted several weeks back in Britain and now I was impatient to get on with the job. I was also increasingly concerned about the impending air strikes and the possible effects on the population of central Bosnia. We had seen in the Gulf War how supposedly precise targeting could still hit innocent civilians.

Eventually Dr Lang called. The convoy was likely to be delayed by the atrocious weather conditions in central Bosnia where thick snow had blocked the roads. He suggested I go with him to an important meeting the following day where there would be various politicians and officials who might be able to help.

It seemed the only alternative. I had tried the Split-based aid organisations but they either did not want to take an outsider or they were not going until the threat of air strikes had passed. The other option of hiring a four-wheel drive vehicle myself and going it alone seemed too reckless even for me.

I joined Dr Lang and his colleagues from Zagreb, including the leader of the Jewish community there, for a chauffeur-driven, police-escorted ride to the meeting. Dr Lang was a heroic figure following his 'white roads' convoy in December. The mission had been fraught with danger throughout but it had ended in success: a lot of people had been brought out and a lot of aid delivered. I described my own experiences and plans and he urged me to press my case with the authorities. I knew however that the one person I had to convince was my first and best ally.

I saw him as I stepped from the car: Ivan Bagaric, his dark figure towering above those beside him. He embraced me in the old bear-like hug but I sensed a distance between us. After a few moments he excused himself and I was left alone to watch the proceedings.

The conference, I knew, was vital – Mate Boban chose it to announce his resignation – but it was all in Serbo-Croat and I could not understand a word. It was also freezing cold and I could not stop shivering despite my warm jacket. I finally managed to corner Ivan at the buffet lunch and with the help of a woman journalist who acted as interpreter tried desperately to convince him of my seriousness.

I was here I said to keep my promise to help the people of Nova Bila. Could I be taken in by his people, perhaps by helicopter? His first reaction was to laugh but I would not be fobbed off. I pressed him again and again throughout the day; by the end of it he agreed to make the necessary enquiries.

There was another dreadful delay of several days while I waited for his decision. My only compensation was Vava who was working in the area and we spoke every day.

At last came the news I wanted to hear: a helicopter was standing by in Posušje to fly me to Nova Bila: we would take off as soon as the weather cleared. I packed my bags and travelled down to Čitluk where I was to await Ivan's further instructions.

Memories flooded back in a rush as I stepped through the hotel doors to a warm welcome from the receptionists and other members of the staff. As I unpacked in a room identical to the one in which Lynne and I had spent so many weeks I could almost hear her voice and those of the Boys, Thierry, Paddy, Sean . . . and of course Collette.

The weather was the opposite of what it had been last summer. Snow lay several inches deep and the temperature was below freezing. Even with three layers of clothes I felt chilled to my bones.

I invited Erna and Stipe to dinner that evening. It was wonderful to see them and to meet the friends they had brought along: a police inspector and his Muslim wife who had been a teacher before the war. I was delighted to see that Erna had put on weight at last. They missed Damir dreadfully but he wrote often and occasionally they could get through to him on the phone.

I took them to the best restaurant in town – one which had

been their favourite before the war robbed them of a decent income – and they enjoyed delicious seafood and good wine for the first time in three years. We talked politics and I caught up on the news: Ivan had arranged for Zoran to deliver mail and parcels to the Muslims so that families could be in touch again; Hafid's wife had had a baby girl and was now living abroad. Erna told me excitedly that Bella, her little dog, had given birth to five puppies. 'The father,' she said seriously, 'has been killed, so she is now a widow!'

As they prepared to leave in the little Renault I had given them months before they wished me luck.

'We have electricity all the time now,' said Erna. 'We'll be able to watch what happens on television.'

Ivan's driver came for me on Monday morning and drove me to Široki Brijeg to pick up Vava. His hugs and jokes lifted my spirits. I had brought him a bottle of Jack Daniels and he opened it even before we arrived at the Ministry of Defence in Posušje.

'Do you think the NATO ultimatum will affect what I'm trying to do?' I asked him.

He laughed loudly. 'It's all talk, as usual,' he said. 'We lost our faith in them long ago. The threats are empty.'

I spent the night with a Croatian family in Posušje. It was even colder there than it had been in Čitluk and my teeth would not stop chattering. In the morning I went to Vava's office to make some calls. I rang the helicopter pilots; I rang my mother who was torn between wanting me to succeed and not wanting me to be in any danger; and I rang Duncan. This would be the last time, I said – at least for a while. I told him I loved him and made him promise to wear a ring I had given him engraved with the symbol of wings shielding the world.

The days dragged by and I thought I would go crazy. Each time I was about to set off a message would come through: fog has come down, we cannot fly. I passed the hours sending messages to Nova Bila and the BIH authorities and fretting over the weather reports. I had never before taken such a keen interest in meteorology.

Finally on February 20 the fog lifted. Five surgeons were travelling with me, who would stay in Nova Bila for a month, and so was Vava which was immensely reassuring. We climbed aboard the big black helicopter at seven in the evening. It was loaded almost to the roof with medical supplies and we had to sit or lie across the boxes as best we could. Vava winked at me from his position beside a huge pack of bandages as the propellers whirred into action.

We flew without lights, unseen but not of course unheard and I tensed as I pictured the anti-aircraft guns below and the damage they could do. The flight took less than forty minutes and we landed in a quarry thick with snow. Quickly the supplies were off-loaded and the patients lifted in on stretchers. With a sudden shock I saw they were all sick and injured adults. Where were the children? I turned to look for Vava but he had disappeared.

The helicopter's blades were turning faster and faster as it prepared for lift-off. I had to make a decision. However sorry I was for these people I had not waited so long and travelled all this way to abandon the children.

I picked up my bag and jumped to the ground. The powerful blades whipped the snow into a blizzard. Icy particles stung my hands and face, half-blinding me. I wiped the snow from my eyes and looked around. I had no idea which way the hospital lay. Only my anger kept me from feeling the cold.

Suddenly Vava appeared out of the darkness. He grasped my freezing hand and helped me to my feet.

'I saw you weren't in the helicopter so I decided to remain behind,' he shouted above the noise of the helicopter rising into the air.

I was enormously relieved but also very suprised that he hadn't left while he could. I knew that he'd survived a terrible episode of the war in Sarajevo. He had been trapped for months amidst the starving people of the besieged city, then under continuous shelling and gunfire from the Serbs. Eventually, after hiding beside the airport for several days, he had managed to escape. Yet here he was risking the same discomfort and danger in a besieged area, though this time the enemy was the surrounding Muslim army.

'Why did you stay?' I shouted back.

'I couldn't just leave you here alone. You don't even speak the language. Ivan would never forgive me,' he replied with a rueful smile.

18

THE PROMISE

We trekked across the quarry, knee deep in snow. At the edge of a field we spotted a vehicle with someone inside. I was relieved to see it was the ambulance which had brought the patients. Now it would take us to the hospital. Vava supposed that our messages had never got through which was why there were no children for the flight.

We were met by the Franciscan doctor who was still wearing his Operation Angel sweatshirt.

'You came back,' he said simply and led us into a warm staff room and an even warmer welcome. To my astonishment one of their phones was working and Vava went off to make some calls while the doctors took me to the ward.

'They have heard you were coming back,' said one of the women doctors. 'It will give them great pleasure to see you have arrived.'

I was not the only arrival. An ITN reporter and cameraman had come to wait for me. Apparently the UN had told them at a briefing a few days earlier that I was due. There was some bad news, however. The gates of the base at Vitez just twenty minutes drive away had been locked and orders given that I was not to be allowed in with the children.

Thankfully I hadn't planned to trek through the snow with the children anyway. All the same I was sad to think that British soldiers would have been forced to turn them away. I realised of course that the order must have come from high above, for the commander had assured me during my last visit that they would give me every assistance.

I was also informed that during the briefing a UN official had stated 'it would be a shame for Becker to grab the limelight!'

I went to each child in turn to explain I had come to take them to safety. A sweet-faced little girl of eleven was lying on one bed, her beautiful long hair spread across the pillow. She had lost both legs in an explosion which had killed her father. Her name was Marija and she smiled up at me.

'Thank you for helping us,' she said softly. 'I have been waiting for two months for the UN to take me away but they have never come.'

The place was packed with patients and relatives who had come to say goodbye. A doctor handed me a list: fifty-five names, twenty-five of them wounded children, the rest brothers and sisters and mothers.

'Will we fit them all on one helicopter?' I asked Vava when he had finished his calls.

'We'll have a damn good try,' he said.

A flight was out of the question that night but a helicopter would fly in the next evening if there was no fog. I resigned myself to yet another delay and went off to sleep in a spare bed in the women doctors' room. It was three in the morning and I was worn out.

In the morning I spotted Elvis, the fixer from Mostar who had turned up with another news crew. His shrapnel wounds had healed well. A couple of hours later a British soldier arrived from Vitez and began to discuss an evacuation with one of the doctors which he said was planned for the next day. The doctor looked at him strangely.

'For months we've been waiting for an evacuation of our patients. How come you arrive now? Would it have anything to do with Sally Becker's presence here?'

'I have my own opinion,' said the soldier, 'but I'm not allowed to state it.' I felt sorry for him; he was only following orders.

The Franciscan who had overheard this conversation could contain himself no longer.

'How dare you,' he cried, 'we've begged and pleaded with you to get our wounded out and nobody wanted to know. Now all of a sudden you're here.'

The soldier asked to see my evacuation list. 'I believe you may have four or five children who are also on the Medivac list. We don't want a mix-up.'

The Franciscan stepped forward: I was to show no list, he said.

'We would rather you took them all yourself tonight. The UN have let us down too often.'

At seven o'clock we gathered the patients together and began transferring them into the ambulances. One little boy who had an external fixator holding the edges of an ugly leg wound together began crying bitterly. He had been orphaned by the war and the nurses had become his family. His screams cut me to the heart but the doctors reassured me that he had an aunt in Split who could look after him.

I had arranged to take everyone to Split because many had relatives there, the hospital was well staffed and well equipped and everyone would speak the same language. I certainly did not fancy another tussle over beds in Britain.

When the ambulances were full Vava and I squeezed inside. Children filled almost every available inch so I half-perched on his knee. He took my hand and gripped it hard for a second or two; it was an emotional moment for both of us. Marija was lying on a stretcher beside me. Every movement made her cry out in pain so I leaned over and gently supported her head with my hands. She met my anxious gaze with the sweetest of smiles. I took my scarf and wrapped it around her neck to keep out the penetrating cold. A baby, dummy clamped firmly in mouth, stared at me, wide-eyed with curiosity.

As the ambulances began to bump and slide along the road to the quarry I looked out of the window. All the staff had come to the doors of the hospital and they waved and waved until we were out of sight. We began the treacherous descent down the side of the quarry and Marija screamed as every jolt sent an agonising spasm through her mutilated body. I gripped her shoulders in a desperate attempt to stop her sliding around and I felt her hand tighten on my wrist as her eyes beseeched me to stop the pain.

At the landing area the patients were taken from the ambulances to a hut built into the hillside. It was hidden from view by the thick snow which covered everything. The only indication of its being there was a spiral of smoke which drifted up from a small chimney in the roof. First came those on stretchers, then the walking wounded, then the relatives. The cold bit into our face and hands and I could feel my toes going numb.

With the patients inside and huddled round the fire, Vava and I stepped outside and scanned the night sky, straining our eyes and ears for the helicopter. Despite the snow it was very dark; we could just make out the silhouettes of the surrounding trees and the lights from the cigarettes of a group of soldiers on guard a few metres away, glowing like fireflies. The wind tore at my bare neck, the cold seemed to pervade every part of my body.

'Will they come, Vava?' I whispered anxiously.

'They promised,' he replied but his voice betrayed his uncertainty.

In the distance I heard the crack of rifle fire and I hoped to God that the doctors were right and that the quarry was hidden from enemy view. Suddenly from out of the darkness four shapes emerged like figures in a dream. As they drew nearer I saw they were two adults and two children. The doctor who had come with us to oversee the evacuation began ushering them away. Vava rushed over to find out what was going on and returned a few minutes later.

Apparently they were a family, a mother and father and their two sons of three and five. The younger boy was in urgent need of a hip operation. He had been on an evacuation list for more than half a year. Now his family had trudged on foot to the quarry in a last desperate bid to get him out. We could not take him, said the hospital doctor, he was not on our list.

The father pleaded for my help. He was not asking for himself, he said, he wanted only for his wife and children to be safe. But the doctor shouted at them and they turned to go back the way they had come. I could not bear their disappointment. I turned to the doctor and offered my own place if he would let them leave. Vava offered his seat as well and I was filled with gratitude for his selfless gesture.

The doctor shrugged: they could wait until everyone was on board and if there was any space left they could have it. I ran after the little family who huddled together for warmth as I explained the situation. The father touched my cheek, his eyes full of tears.

'Thank you,' he said and began tugging the children's woolly hats further down over their ears.

Suddenly one of the soldiers pointed towards the sky and a murmur of anticipation ran round the group. Straining through the darkness we followed the direction of his finger. There was a black shape moving in front of a cloud. The shape flew closer and closer until it took on the outline of a helicopter.

'Thank God,' I breathed.

There were no lights on the helicopter or on the ground but the soldiers ran forward with torches and began to guide it down. When it was almost over their heads the pilot switched on the landing lights and the helicopter settled clumsily on to the snow like a giant bluebottle.

The women came rushing from the shelter, overjoyed by the sight of the machine. Again the blades whipped up a snowstorm and I used my coat to shelter the mother and two little boys. Slivers of ice blew inside my collar and melted into icy rivulets down my back. It took a further hour to unload the supplies while I stamped my feet and rubbed my arms and wondered whether I would ever feel my toes again.

We carried the patients on stretchers in first and the others climbed in after them as the doctor ticked off each name. Finally all those who were on the list were inside but it was a terrible crush. There seemed not an inch of space left. The doctor looked at me and spread his hands. I turned to Vava, desperation on my face.

'I don't think there's room for any of us,' he said despondently but the doctor motioned that we should step in.

'If there's room for me the mother and boys can go instead,' I called.

'OK,' he said and began helping them through the rear door. The woman reached down to her husband, clasping his face in both her hands, and kissed him. I felt a small icy hand slip into mine and I saw it was one of the little boys. I swallowed hard as I lifted him inside. His father ruffled his hair in a last gesture of affection before stepping back.

The doctor insisted Vava and I get in too. I did not see how we could possibly fit in but I edged my way into the crush of bodies. It was pitch black inside the aircraft and cramped to the point of claustrophobia. Arms, legs, feet, elbows pressed against me as I crouched against the cockpit beside Vava, my knees crushing my chest as we guarded the medical records and X-rays of the evacuees. The soldiers heaved and pushed against the mass of bodies as they struggled to close the door.

During those tense and anxious moments nobody made a sound. Suddenly every face was bathed in the glow of a candle held by Marija's mother. Vava whispered a translation as through the light of the flickering flame she began to speak.

'Thanks be to God and all good people. For we are saved.'

Her care-worn face was transfused with a look of peace such as I had never seen.

The pilots strapped themselves in and turned the engines. I gripped Vava's hand in the darkness and prayed that the words of Marija's mother might be true. Slowly the great machine lifted off the ground swaying from side to side as it climbed. I peered at the faces of those closest to me: some were anxious, others were filled with anticipation. Only the babies were oblivious to the danger.

We climbed higher. Time seemed to stand still as we flew

over Bosnia and I kept up my silent entreaty: 'Please let us make it, please, please . . .' The pilot reached out for my hand and I twisted round to him.

'Look there,' he said.

Down below us were the lights of Split like a carpet of jewels in the night. I told Vava who passed the word and suddenly everyone was cheering and laughing and trying to hug one another in that cramped space. Tears streamed down my face as we came in to land and I made no attempt to wipe them away.

I had kept my promise.

AFTERWORD

There are more questions than answers and I suppose there always will be.

I never knew for sure why I got permissions which were denied to others. I never fully got to the bottom of the communications breakdown between the British Government and the UN over the issue of hospital beds. I never untangled the web of misinformation and misunderstanding that bedevilled so many of the messages I sent myself or which were sent on my behalf. I also never discovered why one million pounds worth of medical aid appeared to have been confiscated from Operation Angel or even where it eventually went.

Above all I never really understood why the UN treated me the way they did. Was I merely an embarrassment, or did they resent the publicity that I unwittingly attracted? Individual officers and men were brave and kind and thoughtful – and many of them said supportive words to me in private which they could not say publicly. But the whole is greater than the sum of its parts and for me the whole represented everything that is bad about bureaucracy: inflexible, impersonal and lacking in imagination.

Perhaps it does not matter than I have no answers to my questions: truth as we know is the first casualty of war. What matters is that I was able to overcome the obstacles.

I have had many accolades for what I did and as much criticism. I was accused of being foolish and naïve and of seeking publicity. Such attacks were and still are deeply wounding. I was not looking for fame and if I wanted respect or admiration, well, who does not?

The point is I never set out to become so embroiled in the Bosnian conflict: it just happened that way. Each time I would find myself making a promise which my conscience would then force me to keep. Each time I found myself thinking 'why the hell did I do that' and each time I grew more frightened, knowing what honouring that commitment would entail.

There was nothing special about Bosnia itself to draw me to it. I had never been on holiday there; I had no particular interest in its culture or feeling for its people. I think it was the fact that it seemed so abandoned that drew out the protective instinct in me. That, and the fact that once I was there I found, perhaps for the first time in my life, that I was capable of doing exactly what was expected of me. People took it for granted that I could do these things and so of course I did them.

The memories of it will stay with me always. Sometimes they are as direct as a photograph, other times they come at me obliquely. I often dream now that I am in the sea and a baby is drowning. There are a lot of other people around but for some reason I know I am the only one who can save it. There are all kinds of difficulties in my way and I have to struggle against both the water and my own weariness. But when I wake up I always know that I have succeeded.

I have no children of my own as yet, but I feel I have

contributed to a future generation in some way. Damir, Selma, Elmir, Anton, Marija and all the others can now grow up in peace and have children of their own.

As for Bosnia itself, there is, as I write, peace between Muslim and Croat and the lovely city of Mostar is slowly returning to normal life. But the peace is uneasy and as yet there are no guarantees for the future.

My job there is finished but my work is not yet over. Once I am able to finance operations in the future, Duncan and I hope to assist in other war-torn areas. Having purchased this book you have already contributed to this aim. Sadly there will always be a Bosnia in this troubled world and other innocent children who need our help.